THE FRASER
INSTITUTE

GORDON TULLOCK

THE NEW FEDERALIST

D0400392

The New Federalist

Gordon Tullock

adapted for Canadian readers by
Filip Palda

The Fraser Institute
Vancouver, British Columbia, Canada

Copyright © 1994 by The Fraser Institute. All rights reserved. No part of this book may be reproduced in any manner whatsoever without written permission except in the case of brief quotations embodied in critical articles and reviews.

The author of this book has worked independently and opinions expressed by him, therefore, are his own, and do not necessarily reflect the opinions of the members or the trustees of The Fraser Institute.

Printed in Canada.

Canadian Cataloguing in Publication Data

Tullock, Gordon.

The new federalist

Includes bibliographical references.
ISBN 0-88975-164-1

1. Decentralization in government—Canada. 2. Federal-provincial relations—Canada. 3. Federal government—Canada. 4. Social choice—Canada. I. Palda, Filip (K. Filip). II. Fraser Institute (Vancouver, B.C.). III. Title.
JS113.T84 1994   354.71'07'3   C94-910080-3

Contents

Foreword

GORDON TULLOCK IS A FOUNDER of the intellectual movement known as public choice. Students of public choice believe that the methods of economic analysis should be applied to politics. Forty years ago, when Tullock was beginning his career in economics, this was not deemed to be the best way to understand government. Many scholars put government on a pedestal and considered it a completely efficient instrument for the good. Government could fix things where the market failed. Impartial bureaucrats could be trusted to adjust the money supply, government spending, and taxes in the best interests of voters. Regulations were viewed as the means by which impartial representatives of the people could curb the excesses of private entrepreneurs. Gradually, due to the efforts of a few pioneering scholars, this rosy view came under challenge. Tullock and others suggested that taxes, government spending, and regulations were shaped through bargains and conflicts between interest groups. This idea goes back several hundred years. But the public choice school set it on a firm footing and produced the first evidence that government could be understood as a marketplace, different from others primarily in that in political markets, national actors make claims on property which is not their own.

Several sophisticated insights came from this original idea. The first insight is that the rules which govern the political market will determine how efficient government is at delivering essential services. If a government faces no competition from other political parties, and is able to prevent citizens from leaving, it may allow itself to be inefficient. The Soviet Union was an example of such a government. The second insight is that large governments encourage wasteful lobbying by interest groups. The feeding frenzy of professional lobbyists around national capitals is the most visible part of this waste. Tullock called such waste "rent-seeking." Rent-seeking is easier in large than in small governments because it is difficult for ordinary citizens to see who is preying upon them. Few people have the time or energy to learn how much more they pay for milk because a marketing board has convinced government to give it monopoly rights to the production of milk. Local governments are less plagued by rent-seeking than higher levels of government because citizens have a better idea of what is going on at the local level.

In the present book, Gordon Tullock uses these insights to explain what type of government would be best for Canada. He suggests that we need a smaller central government and that we should give more power to local communities. The traditional argument in favour of a large central government is that there are "economies of scale" in the production of government services. This means that to provide services like public sanitation, roads, a military, and national health, government needs to be big to be efficient. Tullock questions the notion that bigger is better and that we need big organizations to deal with big problems. He guides the reader through many real world examples of small communities which provide most of their needs on their own. Tullock does not deny that there are some services that large governments can provide efficiently, but he notes that these services are a minor part of the business governments have taken on. Today, big government mostly occupies itself taking income from part of society and giving it to another part, and this is not something big governments do better or more efficiently.

Once we accept the notion that bigger may not be better, we can start to ask what might happen if we scattered political power to local governments. The main benefit of decentralizing government power is that it forces politicians and bureaucrats to provide services at a cost that is acceptable to the middle of the road voter. Governments are forced to be efficient because citizens who do not like what they are getting can leave. These departing citizens can move to neighbouring communities that offer a package of tax and services more to their liking. By continually voting with their feet, people put continual pressure on governments to perform. This is democracy at its most direct. It is also informed democracy because the deals that politicians strike with interest groups are easier to spot at lower levels of government. Knowing what your representative is up to is half the game in bringing him to account.

Tullock discusses the merits of privately provided local services such as water, schooling, and fire protection. He suggests that the private market can work well, but that *local* governments may be able to provide these services almost as efficiently. What is crucial is not so much who owns and operates the service as the competitive pressures that the providers face.

The message in this book is one Canadians are not used to hearing. We have been told since Confederation that a strong central government built this country. We continue to be told that we need a strong centre to assure that all Canadians get the same high standard of medicine, schooling, and social programs. Tullock asks us to think about a Canada in which Ottawa, and even the provinces, govern less and in which local communities govern more. More generally he asks us to consider what the best or "optimal" size of government should be. Large governments may be efficient providers of certain services, but they may leave many people dissatisfied. Small governments have a better chance of presiding over a community of like-minded people, but there may not be enough of those people to justify a purely local police force or public sanitation, projects which are only cheap if done on a big scale.

While stimulating us to think about these topics Tullock also gives us an easy-to-understand tour of the major issues in public choice, a field which he has done much to shape over the past forty years. Here is a preview of what the chapters in this book have to say:

Overview of the book

Chapter 1 asks the basic question "what do we want out of government?" Tullock explains that we want a government that is responsive to the people's desires and that also provides services efficiently. These are contradictory aims, and later chapters explain and explore the tensions between these aims.

In Chapter 2 Tullock introduces us to the Sunshine Mountain Ridge Home Owner's association, a community which he refers to throughout the book. This is a private community of homes which provides itself with many of the basic services we are accustomed to believing only a large government can provide. Tullock does not argue that this is the only form of government we need but instead that we need a mix of different governments. This chapter challenges common notions about what governments can do, points out that governments are very flexible, and argues that many of the tasks of higher levels of government can also be taken on by lower levels.

Chapter 3 explains what the right size and mix of governments is. Some things should be done by the central government and others should be left to local councils. The projects a government should look after depend on the economies of scale in completing the projects and also upon how different people's views are about the need for projects. We need large centralized governments only to look after undertakings which it would be too expensive for small governments to look after and on which a substantial consensus exists. Large governments begin to stumble when they take it upon themselves to pass laws on issues on which many people disagree. Language policy is an example of the type of area in which central governments should not meddle.

Chapter 4 suggests that governments need not have a geographic monopoly on all aspects of human relations. That is, the same area should have many different governments doing different things, none of which is subordinate to the other. This is already a fact of life in most democracies but Tullock proposes an original twist on this practice. He proposes that citizens living in the same community should be allowed to choose which government will guide them in certain areas such as marriage, education, and family relations. Catholics could follow the rules of a Catholic government which administered schools, questions of property, and so on. Jews, Muslims, or any other group, be it religious or sociological, should be allowed to govern itself. The reader's first reaction is one of surprise. What if a Jew and Catholic ran their cars into each other? How would they resolve this dispute if they do not follow the same government? Tullock shows us why the schemes he proposes could work. The advantage of such a system of "sociological" governments is that it gives individuals greater choice, and reduces strife between groups.

Chapter 5 explains how democracy, as most people know it, works. Democracy is a mix of trading and ignorance. The trading that goes on in legislatures allows interest groups to help each other out on very different issues. Politicians who represent farming interests will support, say, proposals for inner city building projects, provided inner city politicians support farm subsidies at a later date when they become an issue. The types of deals politicians of differing camps can strike with each other depend on how well ordinary voters are informed about politics. The less well-informed voters are, the easier it is for small, well organized interests to trade in government (i.e., other people's) property. Tullock does not pass judgement on whether the activities of interest groups pressuring politicians to make such bargains are on the whole good or bad. Instead he concentrates on understanding how different types of government structures will influence the role of interest groups.

Chapter 6 continues the survey of democracy begun in chapter 5. The chapter describes and critiques the many kinds of democratic institutions that have been used in both federal and non-federal states. Tullock asks whether legislators should be paid, and what can be done about the political power of government employees. The chapter goes on to consider what effect the threat of losing office has on the performance of elected officials, how different rules within a democracy affect the powers of various interest groups, and the ability of politicians to satisfy the wishes of the majority. Examples of the sorts of rules he considers are the executive veto and the recourse of citizens to referendum.

Chapter 7 dispels two myths about modern government: that large organizations are more efficient than small ones, and that the modern world is so complex that large organizations are necessary. Rather than arguing from theory, Tullock makes his point with a fascinating list of real world examples. He reflects on how big government should be to be an efficient tax collector, protector against crime and war, and supplier of education. He shows that traditional arguments for large government units often have a hidden motive which benefits some special interest group. For example, large school districts with a uniform curriculum and teaching standards benefit teachers at their customers' expense because they give parents nothing to compare their childrens' teachers against. Tullock also explains why increasing complexity does not mean we need bigger government.

Groups will quarrel and have differences no matter whether we have a centralized state or a loose federation of small governments. Chapters 8 and 9 ask how these two different types of government deal with such conflicts. Tullock explains that conflicts arise because jurisdictions overlap or are not clearly defined. This is an important problem with centralized governments but also plagues federations of small governments. If governments or departments were organized to deal only with the problems in their area there would be no conflicts and no need to appeal to higher authorities to make decisions on each specific task of government. Tullock explains that even in loose federations we can get overlaps simply because all the functions of government usually cannot fit into the same area. For example, many of the infrastructures of metropolitan Toronto slop over into Mississauga, a Toronto suburb, and this creates conflicts. Does the existence of such overlaps mean we need a strong central government? Only if the costs of bargaining and coming to a peaceful solution between neighbouring communities is too high. By discussing many examples Tullock gives the reader a feel for when situations with overlaps of authority need strong central government and when they do not.

Chapter 10 summarizes the main themes of the book and repeats Tullock's thesis that decentralized governments are more efficient and better able to adapt to local conditions, and that individual citizens have more control when government is broken down into a number of different units.

A number of people have helped in the production of this book, namely, John Robson, Victor Waese, and Kristin McCahon, all of The Fraser Institute, and I thank them for their kind assistance.

Filip Palda

Preface

by Gordon Tullock

IN THE FALL OF 1990 THE UNITED States Information Service asked me to visit Yugoslavia to give lectures in the capitals of five of the constituent republics. The trip, which was only 6 days long, had the same impact on me that Yugoslavia had on almost everybody. The country seemed to be falling apart. Now in the fall of 1992, the prophecy has been realized, and Russia itself may be following in Yugoslavia's footsteps.

Of course, there is no reason why essentially arbitrary national boundaries are sacred, and there is no *a priori* reason why we should object to Yugoslavia or Russia becoming a set of independent smaller countries. Indeed, officially, both are federated states with individual republics having their own governments. This system was set up under Tito and Stalin when the republics (better called pseudo-republics) were mere subdivisions of an absolute dictatorship. It seems obvious that revisions are needed now.

The reason the pseudo-federal system has not been working well is, of course, to a considerable extent the resentment of some of the republics over what they regard as exploitation by the others, but there is another serious difficulty. In both Russia and

Yugoslavia when they were united nations, people were free to migrate from one part to another. Further, the boundaries between what were essentially internal governmental units were rarely drawn with careful precision to follow ethnic differences. This means that a considerable number of people belonging to one ethnic group are in a "republic" which is dominated by another. At the time of writing, this situation is causing fairly numerous deaths in Yugoslavia and has caused considerable difficulty in Russia, too.

Upon returning from Yugoslavia I decided what we needed was a guide book on how to genuinely federalize the state. This was, I suppose, the standard reaction of a writer. Federalization does not have to be just the "republics". It can and should be carried to a much lower level. Further, the former Russian empire is not alone in potentially benefitting from federal institutions. The older democracies also are best organized federally. The field is one of my specialities, and I decided to produce this book. Although inspired by "Yugoslavia" I think it will be equally useful in the United States, Switzerland, Canada, or, indeed, any democratic country.

I should perhaps warn the reader that this book is not in any real sense the conventional wisdom. There is a new method of approaching politics, called "public choice," in which economic methods are applied to politics. This new method, emphatically, has nothing to do with marxism. I have written much on it elsewhere and will not explain the approach in detail here. For those who want to explore the subject further, Dennis Mueller's *Public Choice II* (Cambridge, 1989) is an excellent introduction.

Nevertheless, this new field is by no means the dominant school of political thought in the United States. In fact, it is still a rather minor part of the average political science department. I myself am confident that we will become the dominant approach eventually. For the time being, however, we are a minority. Thus

I have written this book without much of the technical apparatus of Public Choice. I don't think that members of the more traditional schools of political science will find it either controversial or difficult.

I obviously do not argue that the reader should believe the book because it represents public choice. Indeed, I would say that if the reader finds the book persuasive, this is grounds for believing that public choice is right rather than vice versa.

I also do not think that we have solved all the problems of a federal government; indeed, I do not think we have solved all the problems of government in general. This book, of necessity, is only an introduction. The reader will find that I am frequently less than enthusiastic about various arrangements which I nevertheless recommend.

The explanation for all of this is simple. In the first place, human contrivances rarely work perfectly, and, in the second, we have only been engaged in the scientific study of politics for a relatively short time. I hope that if somebody rewrites this book 100 years from now it will be very much better.

Thus, although I think the advice contained in this book will be of use to anybody attempting to design a federal government, that government will be far from perfect. It will have numerous defects, partly defects which are intrinsic in the problem of combining the preferences of different people, and partly defects which are caused by the fact that we simply do not know as much today as we will know 100 years from now.

In addition to writing this book, I have provided a small bibliography after each chapter except the last. The articles and books have been selected both for their content and their readability. Further, many of them cover considerable ground. Thus some will be found in the bibliography after several chapters. All are worth reading but most readers will be selective and look at only those which meet their immediate needs.

As the reader has already deduced and no doubt will become more firmly convinced as he reads the book, I do indeed believe that most present-day states are too centralized and should become less so. This means movement toward more use of small government units. I think the arguments for this are not just my personal preference, but are very sound products of careful scholarship. I hope that by the time the reader finishes this book he will share my convictions.

Bibliographic note

IT MAY SEEM ECCENTRIC to put a bibliographic note after the Preface, but each of the chapters in this book is to have a brief bibliography of readily available work dealing with the subject of that chapter and we start with the preface.

The basic point of this preface is to discuss *The Federalist Papers* and their relationship to this book. Putting it bluntly, the relationship is not very great, even though I have named it *The New Federalist*. The reason is not that I disagree with John Jay, Alexander Hamilton and James Madison. Indeed, it would take a great deal both of courage and of presumption for any modern scholar to criticize their work. But they were arguing that a specific already-drafted constitution should be adopted by a group of state governments which, once again, already existed. Indeed, in the case of all three of them the constitution was considerably less than what they would have liked.

In those days, "federalist" meant being in favour of strong central government whereas now, in general, it means decentralizing government. All three of the authors were federalists and were arguing for the constitution not because they thought it was ideal but because they thought it was the best that could be done in the situation at the time. Most historians to the present day agree with them in this.

It is not my intent here to disagree with them, or to argue that the Constitution was not indeed a very well-drafted document which can be copied. Indeed it was, by the Swiss. But like the Swiss, I think we can improve on it.

The arguments offered in *The Federalist Papers*, then were devoted to a different problem. They were attempting to produce a more centralized government than the existing 13 independent states. I am suggesting that centralized governments be decentralized. I may end up in somewhat the same place but the arguments are obviously different.

Looked at from the standpoint of today, *The Federalist Papers* are extremely important as a penetrating study of political philosophy. Any modern scholar can benefit from reading them and if any of the readers of this book haven't I recommend that they do. But this book deals with a different problem.

Acknowledgements

THE AUTHOR WISHES TO THANK Samson Kimenyi and Sooyoun Hwang for their assistance. Both of them have done a very careful job of going through the manuscript.

Chapter 1:
Introduction

Views of Federalism

AT THE CLOSE OF THE CONSTITUTIONAL CONVENTION of 1787, John Jay, Alexander Hamilton, and James Madison began writing columns favouring the Constitution, to be published in newspapers under the pseudonym of "The Federalist." These three men were firstly brilliant and secondly deeply immured in philosophy and history. All three of them went on to hold high positions in the United States government created by that Constitution. The citizens of the United States accepted their advice and ratified the Constitution, which is now the oldest surviving written constitution in the world.

At the time there were many other people writing similar columns—sometimes under their own names, sometimes (like these three authors) under a pseudonym. Some favoured the Constitution, some opposed it, but it is the unanimous belief of scholars since that date that "The Federalist" was the best. It has gone through innumerable editions, it is regarded by almost everybody including the Supreme Court of the United States as a basic document in interpreting the Constitution, and it is read with advantage by substantially every single student of political theory in the United States.

The present book, unfortunately, is unlikely to have either the lasting success or even the short run influence of the original. The three authors of *The Federalist Papers* were arguing for the adoption of one specific Constitution. They were not arguing for the general principle of federalism and, indeed, all three of them would actually have preferred a stronger central government than they got. They thought the Constitution was the best that could be done in the concrete circumstances of 1787 America. Americans today have more real admiration for the document than they did then.

Two hundred years have passed since that book was written, and this book is able to draw on the experience and research of the intervening two hundred years. It's surprising how little change that has made. There is, however, another very important difference between *The Federalist Papers* and *The New Federalist*. To repeat, Jay, Hamilton, and Madison were arguing for one particular constitution which was to be a union of 13 already existing sovereign states. Other similar situations have occurred since that period. Canada, of course, is a clearcut case, as are Australia and Switzerland, and there is good reason to hope that Europe will shortly be another.

Nevertheless, "federalism"—that is, having several levels of government dealing with different problems—should not be confined simply to the central government and those large subsections which we call states or provinces. The three authors of the original Federalist knew this and in number 36 discussed "the state within the state." That was not their main interest, however, and they gave relatively little attention to it.

The subsections, or states, in the United States delegate a great part of their governing power to lower level governments usually called counties or municipalities. In Canada the provinces also delegate authority to the municipalities but to a lesser degree than in the U.S. The provinces provide for roughly 40 percent of the budgets of Canadian municipalities (mostly for education) and in recent years have started to take on certain functions traditionally assigned to local government (for example, social services in New Brunswick). This is as much an example of federalism as division of power between the central government and those large parts that we call provinces or states.

This was considered only summarily in the original *Federalist* since that was not what the Constitution dealt with. But local governments and their powers will be an important part of this book. As the reader will discover, we not only will consider the division of power between the states and municipalities. Federalism can also involve smaller local governments and the possibility of parallel governments such as an elected school board in the same location as a city government.

The purpose of government

What is the purpose of government? Ancient philosophers in general thought that it was to establish virtue or do good. Most modern public choice scholars are more modest in their evaluation of government. We simply want government to provide those goods and services that people in fact want and that, for a variety of reasons, are hard to provide through the market. Most people, for example, would like to have the poor taken care of by taxes on those better off. It is true they would have no objection if the poor were taken care of by voluntary contributions, but our experience seems to indicate that voluntary contributions don't produce adequate funds for this purpose. Hence the use of the government to provide that particular service is generally approved. Of course, that does not prove that in general people are in favour of the exact quantity transferred or the methods used by the government.

There is a large literature on why certain types of things, sometimes called public goods, are provided by the market in a very inefficient way and will be provided in a better (although far from optimal) way by the government. This literature will not in general be dealt with to any extent here. We will just accept as a fact that there are a number of things which are better dealt with by the government. We will also accept as a fact that there are other things which are better dealt with by the market. Our discussion here is entirely with the government provision of those goods and services which it provides best.

"Government" as a word is very misleading. Anywhere, even in the most totalitarian dictatorships, there is some decentralization, with some decisions being made at the centre and some out

---

What is the purpose of government?
Ancient philosophers in general thought
that it was to establish virtue or do good . . .

---

at the edge. In the type of government that will be advocated in this book, and which is characteristic of such countries as the United States, Canada, and Switzerland, decentralization is carried further. It's not clear that one really should refer to "the government" in such a country. I personally am subject to quite a number of different governments in different aspects of my life. What will be discussed in this book is how those things should be divided among different "governments."

Many people, particularly in Europe, tend to think that our choice is between being part of a large, centralized nation, or a citizen of a small independent country. Many scholars and politicians crusading for a stronger federal government in Canada have also painted our choices in this stark and limited contrast.

These are not the only possibilities. The author of this book is a citizen of the United States, Arizona, and Pima County. He is also a member of the Sunshine Mountain Ridge Homeowners' Association and lives within the area served by the Tucson Unified School District. All of these are democracies, so he can vote for their higher officials. All of them tax him and provide him with "government" services.

Not only is this a theoretical possibility, but such structures do exist in many countries. It will be one of the points of this book that such a mix provides a much better government than either a centralized government or the breaking up of the large unit into a number of completely independent small units.

In general, we want the government to give the citizens what they themselves want. That, indeed, is the point of democracy. The smaller the government, the smaller the number of its voters. The smaller the number of voters, the more power each individual voter has. That's one side of the argument. On the other side, we have the fact that many government services are hard or impossible for small governmental units to provide. These two arguments have to be set off against each other and since different government activities will turn out to have a different balance, having different governmental sizes is sensible.

The existence of many small government units dealing with certain special problems has another advantage. Not only are these small governments more under the control of their voters in the sense that each individual voter's preferences count for more than in the large government, their existence means that citizens may move from one to the other if they are dissatisfied. If they don't like the schools in downtown Toronto, they can move to its suburb, Scarborough. If they don't like the high school taxes in Scarborough they can move to any one of a number of other suburbs where the schools are not as good as they are in Scarborough, but where taxes are lower.

This is, of course, true internationally as well. It used to be that you could easily tell a Communist country from a capitalist country because the capitalist countries had barriers around their borders to keep people from coming in and "taking jobs." The Communist countries had much more elaborate barriers around their borders to prevent people from leaving. We can all feel very happy that this distinction is apparently on its way to liquidation.

Basically, then, we want a government which is responsive to the people's desires and which provides various services efficiently. A mix of governments is the best way of having this, with certain services dealt with by large centralized organizations and others handled on a very decentralized basis. It realizes the classical Greek meaning of democracy, "the people rule," better than a centralized government, and it's also more efficient.

Bibliography

Bish, Robert L. *The Political Economy of Metropolitan Areas.* A good general treatment of many topics to be covered in this book.

Boadway, Robin. *The Constitutional Division of Powers: An Economic Perspective.* Ottawa: Economic Council of Canada, 1992. A neat summary of the division of powers between different levels in Canada and an economic analysis of the effects of such divisions.

Ostrom, Vincent. *The Political Theory of a Compound Republic: Designing the American Experiment.* Lincoln: University of Nebraska Press, 1987. An excellent study of *The Federalist Papers.*

Tullock, Gordon. *Private Wants, Public Means.* Boston: University Press of America, 1987. An easy introduction to the desirable scope of government.

Tullock, Gordon. *The Economics of Income Redistribution* Boston, Dordrecht and London: Kluwer-Niehoff Publishing, 1983. An easy introduction to a complex problem.

Chapter 2:
The Sunshine Mountain Ridge Homeowners' Association and Other Villages

THE THEME OF THIS BOOK is that government does not have to be monolithic but can be broken down into parts. In fact it will work better if it is. As a beginning, let me talk about a small government segment in which I live, specifically the Sunshine Mountain Ridge Homeowners' Association. This is a cluster of about 250 houses built by a major real estate development company and then sold one at a time. Each owner, when he bought, was required to sign a contract under which he agreed to be a member of the Sunshine Mountain Homeowners' Association, obey its rules and pay an annual fee to it. If he resold, the new owner would also be bound.

In return she would be able to vote for the governing board of this institution, and, of course, have the usual privileges of a citizen in any free state. She can complain to the board, either by going to the regular meetings of the citizens of this little community or circulating petitions, run for office, or organize other people to run for office as a sort of party.

What does this little "government" do? Firstly, we own the streets in this development and maintain them. Shortly after I moved in we resurfaced the main street, which was beginning to show signs of wear. As another significant capital expenditure we have installed a set of new fire hydrants to improve the water supply in case of fire.

The latter is interesting because our fire protection is provided by a private company, Rural Metro. Private companies providing fire protection were pioneered in Arizona and I think there are more here than anywhere else. As part of their fire protection service, they advised us not only to put in these hydrants but exactly how they should be put in and how far apart. Rural Metro is technologically progressive and has invented equipment which permits fire hydrants to be placed twice as far apart as in the more conservative parts of the country.

The Association does a good deal of landscaping with the streets and common areas made to appear, in the view of the homeowners, beautiful. Recently there has been a certain amount of tension about this issue since some of the homeowners think that too much money is being spent on it and other homeowners feel that, if anything, we should spend more. As would be expected in any democracy, there is also a certain amount of complaining with the householders in one small part of the community, possibly even just one householder, claiming that the landscaping in their area should be changed one way or another.

We also have recreational facilities. There are two swimming pools, and the issue as to whether both or only one should be heated in the winter has been widely canvassed. We also have a set of tennis courts and areas where large parties can be held under shelter or barbecues held out in the open.

We also have some police protection of our own. Basically we depend on the Pima County Sheriff's Office to provide us with police protection, but arrangements were made with a private police protection agency to supplement the Pima County Sheriff's Office during that part of the night in which it was thought that we might have an exceptional security problem.

We also have general laws. The general appearance of the development when it was sold by the company was very attractive. In order to retain this beauty, there are rules about the kind of gardening that can be done in that part of a house that is visible from the street. We are also prohibited from anything extreme in the way of changing the external appearance of our house. Nobody, I think, is much interested in doing this since the houses are quite handsome, but if we get some eccentric who would like to paint his house purple, he can be stopped.

The traditional form of government in China, indeed in most of Asia except the Islamic part, provides for the local villages being self-governing. Strictly speaking, large cities are federations of local villages.

All of this is organized by contract and all of the people living in the area knew about the contract when they moved in, so they are in general reasonably satisfied. As in any democratic organization there are squabbles and tensions, but they're not particularly severe.

Now that I have told you what we do for ourselves, what do other people do? The first thing to be said, of course, is that although we are not formally part of the local government, the local government treats us as if we were. The reason for this is simple and straightforward. The elected board representing 500 voters can talk to the members of the County Board of Superintendents[1] and they will be listened to. Five hundred voters have clout. Indeed, one of the characteristics of this small "government" which it shares with the other "local" governments is the ability to effectively lobby with higher level agencies. This will be discussed in considerable detail in Chapter 4.

As a particular example of this, the Sunshine Mountain Ridge Homeowners' Association is only one of a considerable number of somewhat similar developments being put up by the same company, Fairfield, in the immediate area.

What other things do we leave to others? I mentioned earlier that we depend basically on the Pima County Sheriff's Department for our police protection, and once again the fact that the council represents 500 voters means we get very good protection. As I also mentioned, we decided that it was not quite good enough and we wanted even more protection, so we hired additional patrol service from a specialized company.

In many parts of the United States associations like ours would depend on the city or county for fire protection. The reason we depend on a private company is essentially the fact that we're located in Arizona where such private companies abound. In our case, the actual protection contract is negotiated by the homeowners' association rather than the individuals, although we are billed individually.

There are other things that we obtain from outside, of course. As mentioned above we maintain our own roads, and for this purpose we normally contract out to some small private companies in that business. This, as a matter of fact, is what the city and county governments also do when they're maintaining roads, and we frequently use the same companies.

---

1   This is a county and therefore we have superintendents instead of aldermen.

There is also the matter of water and sewage disposal, which we buy from a local government agency. It's rather common in the United States for sewage disposal and water to be provided by the same organization with one bill. The reason is probably that sewage disposal is roughly correlated with water consumption, and hence this is simpler. The individual householder is billed for this service.

There are a few other utilities which we buy from private companies—our houses all have gas and electricity and those who wish to have cable television. In all three cases this is bought from private companies. Our rubbish is collected by a company which has a contract with the association. Here, again, we are billed individually. Landscaping of our common areas and roads is taken care of by a private company under contract with the association.

There are many more important government services we obtain from outside. We do have our own road system inside the development but most of us drive far more miles per day on the main road system of the city and county. It appears that most people, if given their choice, would like to live on a quiet road in which cars drive slowly enough so that children are not in any great danger. They also would like to be close to a major road network so that it doesn't take very long to get to shops, place of work, etc. In our case, there's a division of labour, with the Association providing the local streets and the main streets being provided by higher levels of government.

We are, as I mentioned, dependent on the sheriff's office of Pima County for basic police protection, but there are other higher level, more specialized, police forces also involved. The State Police Force can be called if necessary and the federal government has the FBI and several highly specialized police forces which also offer us some protection.

There are, of course, many, many other areas where higher level governments provide services. The military is an obvious case, but such minor matters as the patent office and the weather service are national. We could go on with an almost endless list. We shall see later that it's not obvious that all of these things should be carried out by the level of government at which they are presently located, but nevertheless most of them are not suitable for the Sunshine Mountain Ridge Homeowners' Association.

This book is not a plea for the existence of very small local governments, but for a meld of different sized governments. It is the most efficient way to run a state.

I should finally close with one other aspect of the Sunshine Mountain Ridge Homeowners' Association. That is that the population is rather homogenous. Fairfield is a company with a great deal of experience in this kind of thing. It has constructed a whole series of these homeowners' associations, a number of them on the same former ranch as the Sunshine Mountain Ridge Homeowners' Association. They designed them to attract a different type of family in each. It seems that people, on the whole, like living with other people who are similar to them.

Thus there are practically no children in Sunshine Mountain Ridge Homeowners' Association, but down below us in the valley there is another somewhat similar development in which practically every family has children. Income levels also have some affect on segregation. The Sunshine Mountain Homeowners' Association is the most expensive of the ones in this immediate area although there are several others that are very close. This similarity in the people who live in each association tends to lead to the association being more in accord with its members' preferences. The fact that you can vote with your feet provides an additional element both of freedom and of efficiency.

This homogeneity is emphatically not true of Pima County and Tucson, an area where almost ⅓ of the population is Mexican.

The Sunshine Mountain Ridge type of homogeneous "government" is quite common in the United States. For the past 20 years I have always lived in something like this. The most recent one, in Washington D.C., was a very large apartment building owned by its "tenants."

This type of government is also very old. As some of you may know, I was at one time a China specialist. The traditional form of government in China, indeed in most of Asia except the Islamic part, provides for the local villages, the analogues of the Sunshine Mountain Ridge Association, being self-governing. Strictly speaking, large cities are federations of local villages. Since these local self-governments have strong democratic overtones, although not normally run as perfect democracies, and coexisted for the last 2 or 3 thousand years with a highly despotic central government, they were probably the most efficient part of the government.

They are also proof that decentralized localized governments of the sort represented by the Sunshine Mountain Ridge Homeowners' Association, or a street "government" in Peking, are highly flexible and do not require anything very special about the other levels of government. This book is not a plea for the existence of very small local governments, but for a meld of different sized governments. It is the most efficient way to run a state.

Bibliography

Bish, Robert L. and Vincent Ostrom. *Understanding Urban Government—Metropolitan Reform Reconsidered.* Washington, D.C.: American Enterprise Institute for Public Policy Research, 1973, p. 111. This work provides a brief introduction to the public choice approach to public administration, the provision of education, police and fire protection and intergovernmental organization.

Bish, Robert L. and Hugh O Nourse. *Urban Economics and Policy Analysis.* New York: McGraw-Hill, Inc., 1975, pp. 109-140 and 175-216, 323-352. More on public goods, political organization, and privatization and contracting.

Fixler, Phil E. Jr. and Edward C Hayes. "Contracting out for Local Public Services," in *The Hidden Wealth of Cities: Policy and Productivity Methods for American Local Governments.* Edward C. Hayes, ed. JAI Press, 1989. A survey of degrees and types of privatization and contracting for provision of public goods and services. The end of the chapter includes a list of research organizations on contracting and privatization.

Heung, Raymond. *The Do's and Don'ts of Housing Policy.* Vancouver: The Fraser Institute, 1976. A discussion of Canadian housing policy and the degree of higher government control over how communities are organized.

Olson, Mancur. *The Logic of Collective Action.* Cambridge: Harvard University Press, 1965. A fundamental discussion of pressure groups. He does not include lower level governments in his survey, but they fit his analysis perfectly.

Walker, Michael A., ed. *Privatization: Tactics and Techniques.* Vancouver: The Fraser Institute, 1988. A discussion about the comparative costs of government and the private provision of local services.

Chapter 3:
Why Do We Have Some Things Done by Government, and Which Governments Should Do Them?

A mix of governments

IN THE MIDDLE YEARS OF THIS CENTURY most economists held that when the market did not work perfectly one should logically call in the government. Back in the '50s and early '60s these people had a hidden assumption that the government was perfect. Of course the government is not perfect and hence the line of reasoning was false.

It should be said that there is a group of people whom I call American anarchists, although the heresy is spreading to Europe, who do the opposite. They prove that some part of the government works badly and then urge that the private market take over. These people are radical, thinking that we should have private police forces, private armies, etc. They're making the same mistake with opposite sign. Human institutions are imperfect, government is imperfect, and the market is imperfect, because humans are imperfect. It is wise to select the best among a number of possible alternatives, none of which is perfect.

The theme of this book is that, on the whole, government works best if we have a mix of different levels instead of a single centralized government. Further, we will argue that this system makes it possible to have geographically larger government units at the top level than one would expect if the whole government were a unified block. Different levels of government dealing with different problems is the ideal. Only the relatively thin collection of activities subject to large economies of scale need a central government.

As we will see below, there is a pretty general rule that tells you which type of government should deal with each individual subject. Note that this is a general rule; it will not fit perfectly. Further, if we had a separate level of government for every activity we might be members of 7,000 or 8,000 different governments. Under the circumstances, it is sensible to bundle them together. This reduces the difficulty the voter faces in supervising his servants, but in itself brings in a certain amount of inefficiency.

I shall frequently refer to the United States and Canada, but it should be emphasized that both of these countries, although an illustration, are far from having ideal governments. Switzerland, in my opinion, comes closer to the ideal, but once again is far from perfect. I hope that new governments may do better than either of these.

When I was talking about my ideal government in Zagreb, one of the members of the audience protested that my vision was suitable only for advanced countries and not for backward places like Yugoslavia. Actually, Yugoslavia is not as backward as he implied, but the fact remains that the basic structure I am going to describe was characteristic of the area that is now the United

States way back in colonial days. A variant of it was characteristic both of the empire of Alexander the Great and of the Roman Empire. The British in India had a bizarre variant on the scheme in which a good deal of the local government was handled by hereditary princes. It doesn't require high economic development. Indeed, it's easier for less developed countries than a truly centralized government would be.

. . . government works best if we have a mix of different levels instead of a single centralized government.

The reader should take warning that the outcome will not be perfect, only better than the alternatives. We must also talk a little bit about what the objectives of government are. As a characteristic of human life, only individuals make decisions.

Individual preferences and majority vote

We are thrown back to individuals trying to do as well as they can for themselves. The individual could, of course, be an hereditary monarch, a fairly nasty dictator, somebody who is trying to make up his mind whether he should buy a Toyota, or the voter in a democracy. In all cases a decision will in fact be made by that person and his objective will be to do as well as he can in that decision.

Now to say that he means to do as well as he can does not mean that he must be "selfish." All of us occasionally make gifts to charity. Some of us far more often than occasionally. Almost all of us have sometimes made decisions which we think are morally right even though in material terms they are to our disadvantage. This is not an argument that people behave selfishly, only that we recognize that the ultimate decisions are always made by people and those people always make the decisions in terms of what they think is desirable.

When we say that individuals make these choices, it should be emphasized that in many cases the individual's choice must be melded with those of a number of other people in order to effect the ultimate decision. I have a perfect right to buy any car I want, and in Tucson, my home city, there are a number of agencies from many automobile companies. In addition, I can order from out of town if I want something special, say a Maserati. Further, there is a large selection of used cars to choose from. I make my own decision at this level.

But at another level, my decision is affected by other people. The designers of these cars must sell them to many people and so they try to make them attractive to a large number of people. Of course, some of the designers of these cars are trying to attract special groups of people and others have much wider targets. As a result, I do have genuine choice and quite a large choice. Nonetheless, if everyone else decides they want cars on three wheels I will have to buy a three-wheel car myself even if I prefer a four-wheel car. There is, of course, the alternative of accepting the immense cost of having a special four-wheel car made for myself.

The influence of other people on the outcome, the problem of my decision being effected strongly by other people's decisions, is even more severe in politics. In a democratic government, almost uniformly, I have to have my vote combined with others to make a decision. There are times in democracies where a simple majority of the voters is required. It is also, however, not particularly uncommon that something larger than a majority is required and, under some circumstances, less than a majority.[2]

---

2   Margaret Thatcher got much less than a majority in each of her elections.

Amendments to the American Constitution require very much more than a simple majority and the most common single voting body in the United States is a jury, which traditionally had to vote unanimously. In those states where it does not have to vote unanimously, it nevertheless requires far more than a simple majority. Switzerland, on the other hand, is very majoritarian. Canada has an exotic formula for constitutional amendments, requiring approval from the national Parliament and seven of the ten provinces, provided that those provinces are home to at least 50 percent of the country's population.

My desire as to exactly what policies I would like to have the government carry out are important only to the degree that at least some other people share them. This is unfortunate, but a compensation for that is the fact that other people have to make at least some efforts to get their choices in line with mine.

In any event, in the rest of this book we shall assume that the objective of government is simply to do what the people want. In general we shall assume that is best achieved by following a majority although anyone who has read my other books knows that I regard simple majority voting, though certainly better than dictatorship, as something that can be improved on.[3]

Indeed this has been characteristic of British governments in the twentieth century. Lincoln and Wilson were both elected with much less than a majority of popular votes. And there is a case to be made that John Kennedy was elected President of the United States with fewer popular votes than his rival, Richard Nixon. Due to some confusion over the vote in Alabama, most standard references show Kennedy as having a few more popular votes than Nixon. For more on this interesting controversy, see my letter to the editor and Francis Russell's reply in *The New York Review of Books*, Vol. XXXV, No. 17, November 10, 1988.

3   See *The Calculus of Consent: Logical Foundations of a Constitutional Democracy* with James M. Buchanan, (Ann Arbor: University of Michigan Press, 1962), and "A New and Improved Method of Voting" with Nicholas Tideman, *Journal of Political Economy*, 84, No. 6, October 1976, pp. 1145-59.

In a two-house legislature where the election method is different in the two houses, a majority requirement in both houses is equivalent to requiring something more than majority in one house. Exactly how much depends on the institutions. If you have, as the United States does, a veto from the President which can only be overridden by ⅔ in both houses, the equivalent is even higher. I am in favour of all of these things and would recommend them to my readers. But that is not the purpose of this book. The purpose of this book is to deal with how government should be divided among different levels that are purely majoritarian.

Small constituencies versus economies of scale

In general, the fewer people voters must meld their preferences with, the more likely they are to be satisfied.[4] The explanation is very simple. If I make the decision myself, it is my decision. If I make it in a voting body of 5, my influence on the outcome is at best about 20 percent. If I make it in a voting body of 70 million, my influence in that decision shrinks to a very, very small figure.

This, if it was the only thing to be considered, would suggest that we do everything by the market and prohibit mass production because mass production tends to produce products which are designed to satisfy a lot of people instead of one. Obviously we're not going to do that. There are countervailing factors.

The basic countervailing factor is economy of scale in the market. We can simply produce cars very, very much more

---

4   See my "Social Cost and Government Action," *American Economic Review*, 59, May 1969, pp. 189-97. A mildly revised version was reprinted in my *Private Wants, Public Means: An Economic Analysis of the Desirable Scope of Government*, (New York: Basic Books, Inc., 1970), pp. 2-28. Reprinted by University Press of America, New York, 1989.

cheaply if we produce a lot of them that are just alike than if we produce a set, each one of which is unique. I saw a picture of the Vanderbilt family in the early part of this century and they had a matched set of cars from a tiny one for their five-year-old (I presume it was not fast enough to be a danger), through a series of larger ones to the largest, that of Mr. Vanderbilt himself. They were of course very wealthy people. I've seen another set of somewhat similar cars which were kept by Khrushchev at his villa in the Crimea. Apparently in this case they were primarily for grandchildren. He also, of course, was a very, very wealthy man although his wealth was invested in something—political power—which was not as secure as Vanderbilt's railroads.

The same economy of scale phenomenon exists in government. The traditional example here is the military, because there are very pronounced economies of scale in armies. On the whole, the big army beats the small one. I think, however, a better example is simply the road net. I want to drive many places and no doubt could design a road net which met my preferences better than the one which I confront in Tucson. The cost of providing everybody with their own road net, however, is obviously so utterly impossible that no one has ever seriously considered it.

There are many other areas where it is convenient to have the wishes of many people melded instead of satisfied one by one. Sewage disposal and water supply, to take two very local activities, are subject to very pronounced economies of scale and although it would not be impossible for the citizens of Tucson to provide their own water,[5] no one thinks of it because of the immense cost. In this case there are also economies of scope; in

---

5 Tucson happens to lie on top of a very large although very deep aquifer. Septic tanks which did not contaminate the aquifer could be designed, but they are expensive.

other words, it is more economical to combine the water and sewage facilities under the same body.

In government, there are a number of other activities in which not only are there economies of scale, but also what I would say are "economies of area." Air pollution control, for example, with present technology, is simply impossible on the level of individuals. I don't want to claim that somebody some day might not invent a gadget that permits me personally to control the purity of the air that I breathe when I am outside. But even in the unlikely event that they do, it would almost certainly be far more expensive than using governmental means.

Many government activities have this characteristic. The police would find it quite difficult, for example, to provide protection for one house without at least stopping and interrogating suspicious characters they found in the neighbourhood. If they did that, they would automatically be providing protection for others. I mentioned the economies of scale of water and sewage. They are cheapest if there is at least some contiguity between the different areas served.[6]

Externalities

There are also, loosely speaking, economies of scale in dealing with what are known as "externalities." Sometimes the activities of a certain group of people will harm a different group. For a very simple example, if I were to paint my house purple the rest of the Sunshine Mountain Ridge homeowners would object. I would be, by my own decision, doing something that satisfies me but inflicts cost on them. This is called an externality. In contain-

---

6   The continuity doesn't have to be complete. We have a small part of the city of Tucson which used to be a suburb and does indeed have its own water and sewage system. But it is likely that with time this will be merged into the main system.

ing this sort of cost, larger governmental units have a certain advantage.

Externalities can be negative, as the above example shows, or positive. For example, the next two houses on my east side are occupied by retired people who are fanatical gardeners. In consequence, I gain the opportunity to look over very pretty yards. This is a positive externality from their private decisions.[7]

Almost everything we do has at least some effects on other people. I wear neckties. Although it is primarily simply a matter of habit, if I had to justify it, I would say that I wear them because of their effect on other people. It gives them the impression that I have good taste (I hope).[8] Traditionally, these external effects have been the basic reason that we have government activity.

It is hard for most moderns to believe, but most governments through history have in fact controlled people's clothing by what are called sumptuary laws. Even today there is a little bit of this sort of thing as the reader can readily find out for himself by attempting to walk naked through a main part of his city. But mainly, today we make no effort to control such insignificant externalities.

There are many business activities which are indulged in by corporations or by individual entrepreneurs that produce significant external costs. The obvious case is air and water pollution. Road congestion and noise are mainly produced by non-business activities, but business also contributes. Most crimes are cases in

---

7   The new owner of the house on my west shows signs of also developing into a fanatic gardener. If so I will receive positive externalities from gardens on both sides. I will also, however, receive negative externalities from the fact that my ordinary garden will show up as a gap in a row of outstanding ones.

8   Some of them develop the impression that I am a stuffed shirt.

which the victim can reasonably regard himself as subject to a negative externality.

Positive externalities which require government activity are normally things which an individual would not undertake on his own. Very early in this literature I used "mosquito abatement" as an example. The mosquito is a major pest in most of the United States and it is quite possible for individuals to keep them under control within their home either by screens on all the windows or, if you have air conditioning, by simply keeping the windows closed. Keeping the mosquitoes from making your garden very unpleasant in the early evening is in general, however, something that is very, very difficult or impossible to do on an individual basis. It is not particularly difficult to do actively by a sizeable government unit although this will not be able literally to get rid of all of them. You can only reduce the nuisance sharply.[9]

There are many other government services which we would simply not provide for ourselves if we did not have the instrumentality of some kind of collective agency. It is the general view of economists that this is the basic justification for government. We are trying to give people what they want insofar as possible and we use the market where we can and the government where it works better. Remember, as we have said above, that most everything develops at least some externality. It is not obvious that we would switch to the government for almost everything.

Intergovernmental externalities

If one examines the history of almost any two governments which happen to be adjacent, whether they are tiny suburbs or great

---

9   Currently, environmentalists sometimes object to doing this on the grounds that they are part of the natural environment. Most environmentalists don't, however, because this is part of the natural environment they really don't like.

nations, you'll quickly find cases in which the two governments are fairly strongly in disagreement as to some kind of activity that takes place near their border. Bangladesh and India have had fairly violent quarrels about certain rivers. The United States and Canada have had some heated, although not really violent, disputes over fishing boundaries on the Atlantic coast.

As a general rule, people find that they are more likely to have the government policy in direct accord with their preferences, the smaller the government unit that they are in.

Almost any government, if you look at it carefully, will be found to have a series of squabbles even between its different branches. In Ontario the state-owned hydroelectric company, which is the largest of its kind in North America, is constantly having run-ins with the province's ministry of the environment.

This kind of friction between different parts of the same government or, for that matter, between different parts of General Motors, is inevitable in human life. They are externalities that cannot be totally eliminated. *In designing any given organization we try to arrange the different divisions in such a way that those who generate large externalities on each other are under the control of the same superior.* Thus, it is hoped, that superior can mediate the difficulties or arrange things so that the structure has fewer undesirable externalities than it otherwise would. They never do this perfectly, but then, as we have said several times, human institutions are imperfect.

The median voter

I would like to restate the arguments of the previous sections, to show more precisely why there is a tension between what the individual wants and the benefits to all from scale economies.

If we temporarily ignore economies of scale, the smaller the government unit dealing with any given problem the more likely that it will please a given citizen. The point can be fairly easily demonstrated; let me do so by using a bit of political technology called "the median preference theorem." Suppose we are considering the level of air pollution that will be permitted in a given city. In reducing air pollution the question is, in essence, how many resources we want to spend. The more we spend, the less the pollution, but also the less we have to spend on other things.

Figure 1 shows the choice continuum. On the right we spend very large resources, so the only pollution left is that of human breath.[10] On the left there are no resources spent on air pollution control. We thus have low taxes, and a high level of asthma, lung cancer, etc.

Most people will regard some position on this line as an optimum and their satisfaction will fall off as you move away from that particular optimum. Figure 1 shows three individual voters. Normally, of course, there would be many more. The tent-shaped figures show that each one has an optimum and their preferences fall off as you move away. The degree of satisfaction with clean air rises up to a certain point for each voter. But past a point the voter feels that she is giving up too much in other government services and the degree of satisfaction from pollution abatement falls.

---

10   Reducing air pollution to zero would require that you stop breathing. Human breath with its accompanying collection of germs is one of the more dangerous sources of air pollution. Fortunately, it's a very small one.

Figure 1: Resources Devoted to Air Pollution Reduction

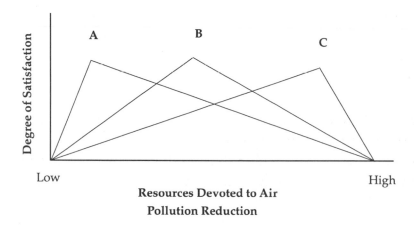

Duncan Black pointed out that the preference of the middle or "median" voter can always get a majority against any other proposal. If there are three voters the B optimum would get a two to one vote against either A or C. If we had 70 million and one voters the median preference would always get at least 35 million plus one votes against any alternative.

In the real world, of course, things are usually not arranged in this unidimensional pattern but a great deal of research has indicated that this model nevertheless is a good approximation. There still is a median and it still has a dominant position. We use it here because other more complex models would lead to the same conclusions.

Suppose we divide our group into smaller groups. If we could divide them in such a way that those on the left are in one group and those on the right are in the other, both of them could be very markedly more satisfied. Obviously it won't be possible to do that all the time.

Let us go to the other extreme and assume that we divide into two groups with people assigned to each one of the groups randomly. In this event it would still be true that the average person would be closer to the median voter in his particular new group than he was to the median voter in the old group.[11] The difference would, however, be small.

These rules apply no matter what the size of the group. In the extreme where the group becomes one person, then everybody is perfectly satisfied. This phenomenon must be set off against the economies of scale in generating pollution reduction or other externalities. Or for that matter increasing the positive externalities.

As a general rule, people find that they are more likely to have the government policy in direct accord with their preferences, the smaller the government unit that they are in. On the other hand, the various economies which lead us to create the government to begin with instead of relying on the market are smaller the smaller the government. Put differently, the smaller the government the more things which occur within it affect outsiders. Conversely, the smaller the government, the more its citizens are effected by the activities of "foreigners." In deciding on the optimal size of government we balance these two factors off against each other.

But note that it is very unlikely that we will get a perfect balance. Different people will disagree as to exactly what the balance should be. Nevertheless, the objective is fairly straightforward. We should, as far as possible, reduce the size of government until the gains at the margin that we get from having governments that are more in accord with the preferences of their citizens are counterbalanced by the marginal losses we get from reduced economies of scale.

---

11 For those readers for whom this is not intuitively obvious, it is formally proved in Yoram Barzel, "Two Propositions on the Optimal Level of Producing Public Goods," *Public Choice* 6 Spring 1969, pp. 31-7.

Two further benefits of small government

So far I have explained that the prime benefit of having a small government is that it accurately reflects the preferences of voters. There are two less obvious benefits which need to be mentioned and discussed. The first is that small governments allow people to "vote with their feet." The second benefit is that information is easier to absorb under a small government. Both of these are benefits because they allow voters to exercise control over their leaders.

Voting with your feet

As I mentioned in Chapter 1, one traditional way of telling whether one was in a Communist country or not was to look at the borders. If the border was carefully guarded to prevent the citizens from leaving you were in a Communist country. If the border was either unguarded or guarded to prevent foreigners from entering you were in a non-Communist country. The whole point of the wall dividing Germany was to prevent the Germans from voting with their feet and the moment the wall came down it was obvious that the East German government could not much longer exist.[12]

The development of almost free immigration inside the European common market has had somewhat the same effect. Indeed, the Brussels bureaucracy is now busily trying to get the various countries to adopt identical rules in many areas in order to set up

---

12   Due to some odd developments in my life, I once had dinner with the head of the American Communist Party. He had just returned from East Germany and it was just after the wall was built. He explained to me at some length that the wall had made an immense improvement in the spirit of East Germany—as he put it, "Nation building was impossible before." I responded: "Of course. A prison without walls won't work."

a sort of cartel in which there is no voting-by-foot, in other words, no competition. This is one of the better arguments against the confederation, but should be regarded also as an argument against the Brussels bureaucracy. It is to be hoped that at least one of the countries has sense enough not to participate in the cartel.

The same forces are also at powerfully at work within Canada. Every policymaker agrees that barriers to the movement of workers between the provinces are bad, but these barriers persist in the hundreds. And while the governments may "compete" through the regulations, they conspire together to allow each to trap its current inhabitants. An undertaker trained in Ontario cannot practice in Quebec without training there first for twelve months. Provincial governments procure services from local workers even if out-of-province workers can offer a better price. The federal government in the meanwhile anaesthetizes the provinces against the consequences of their restrictive practices by granting large transfers. Workers are surprisingly mobile for a country as thinly populated as Canada and it is interesting to speculate how much more mobility there would be without these provincial barriers to movement.

In the United States, where many states are as large in geographic extent and population as a good many nations, the migration from state to state is also important. State governments frequently discuss these issues. The legislature will change the law in hopes of attracting industry and workers. In general, there is competitive pressure on these local governments.

All of this, although it does look like the private market for commodities, has one significant difference. There is no residual claimant, no owner, of the state.[13]

---

13   It seems likely that up to the unification of Germany and Italy we did have something rather like privately owned small governments with free migration. An article by Backhaus and Wagner on the situation in Germany

There are, of course, certain interests in any community which act somewhat like proprietors. The bureaucrats and owners of sizeable tracts of land are obvious examples. Indeed, most people involved in real estate also are interested in attracting immigrants. These groups are far from the voting majority and hence the local governments do not put as much effort into attracting immigrants or being nice places to move into as would a private proprietorship.

Since the reason they do not put all these efforts in is that the citizens are permitted to vote democratically, it is not obvious whether this is an advantage or a disadvantage. It may be that we would not like the situation in which we could freely move from one government to another and the governments would be run in a profit maximizing way. On the other hand, there is at least one scholar, Spencer MacCallum,[14] who argues most strenuously that such a system would be better. It would seem likely that careful historical studies of Germany and Italy before the unification would solve the problem.

But the problem that we deal with here is not proprietary governments that we're not likely to have, but democratic governments. And in democracy, the possibility of migrating from one area to another provides the individual citizen an additional element of control over the government within which he lives.

---

argues that the princelings who operated in Germany had little or no monopoly power. They found themselves compelled, no doubt contrary to their desire, to run attractive governments in order to keep their citizens from migrating to the next Duchy over. (See Jurgen Backhaus and Richard E. Wagner, "The Cameralists: A Public Choice Perspective," *Public Choice* 53, p. 3-20, 1987).

14   Spencer MacCallum, "The Social Nature of Ownership" in *Modern Age*, Vol. 9, No. 1, 1964, p. 49-61.

The addition of voting with your feet to voting with a ballot is a significant improvement.[15]

It can be seen that there are a number of problems here which will in fact be discussed in greater length in the rest of the book. The problem is to set off the advantages in terms of giving people governments which are trying to maximize their preferences as opposed to that of someone else on the one hand, and the various externalities which make very small governments impractical for many activities on the other hand. What mix in governments is optimal and exactly how that mix would operate is the subject of this book.

Getting information to the voter

As another complication, we have the problem of the voters. The voters themselves normally do not want to take too much time voting. It's easy to demonstrate that, particularly when there are a lot of voters, the individual's vote has very little influence on the outcome although the outcome of course is determined by all the individuals together. Under the circumstances, individuals almost never devote much effort into becoming informed or, for that matter, voting. In fact, individuals frequently do not vote at all. In some ways a rather low voter turnout—50 percent or so—is a sign of maturity in democracies. Countries that have been democracies for a long time tend to have low voter turnouts.

The information problem is somewhat more difficult. Very local governments—like my Sunshine Mountain Ridge Homeowners' Association—are cases in which it is very easy indeed for anyone who wishes to become informed about the people who are "running" for office. Indeed, in many cases you

---

15   This general theory is normally called "the Tiebout effect." Tiebout mainly examined the area around large American cities, but the phenomenon is universal.

know them personally. Heads of state get an immense amount of publicity and so do their opponents in any given election. Under the circumstances it's easy to learn at least something about them; in fact it's extremely difficult if you want to avoid any information.

Democratic governments may not fulfil all the dreams of the philosophers, but they do a moderately good job. The same cannot be said of dictatorships.

Unfortunately, intermediate cases, and they are in many ways the most important, are harder to get information on. Newspapers, TV stations and radio stations actually pay much less attention to local government than to the national government.

On the other hand, the larger local governments are sufficiently removed from many people so that they have little personal contact. The consequence is that in the U.S. the information is probably at its worst at the city, county, and perhaps state government levels and at its best at the two extremes. This should be taken into account in designing your government. In Canada there is a high level of publicity about senior figures in provincial governments, which is probably explained by the relatively greater control over resources provinces have compared to their counterparts, the American state governments.

Unfortunately, information held by voters about government tends to be rather asymmetrical. The individual who cannot name his member of parliament or his congressman will know a good deal about various government programs that directly affect him. If he is a farmer, he will be reasonably well informed about the farm program. The ordinary citizen may have strong opinions about the exact location of a highway extension that is to be built near his residence or about the desirability of protective tariffs so he can make more money in his occupation than he could if Koreans were permitted to export more to North America, etc.

Since the areas where he has more information are usually the areas where he is specially interested, he is apt to have more influence there than elsewhere. In general, this phenomenon is perverse. A vote-maximizing democratic government will pay more attention to small groups of well-informed voters who are likely to remember it at the next election than to ill-informed voters, even if the latter are more numerous. Nevertheless, it seems to be something that cannot be avoided in a democracy.

However, it seems to be worse in dictatorships. So I end this chapter as I began it—by pointing out that we cannot expect perfection in human institutions. I am sure the chapter has convinced the reader that government is indeed far from perfect. Nevertheless, we must do the best we can with the tools we have. Democratic governments may not fulfil all the dreams of the philosophers, but they do a moderately good job. The same cannot be said of dictatorships.

Bibliography

Black, Duncan. *The Theory of Committees and Elections.* Boston, Dordrecht and London: Kluwer Academic Publishers, 1987. A quantitative presentation of optimal voting strategies and arrangements.

Olson, Mancur. *The Logic of Collective Action: Public Goods and the Theory of Groups.* Cambridge: Harvard University Press, 1965, pp. 1-65. An excellent discussion of the dynamics of size in groups and organizations. If individual self-interested behaviour is assumed, what are the implications or even the possibilities of promoting a common interest among individuals?

Ostrom, Elinor. *Governing the Commons—The Evolution of Institutions for Collective Action.* Cambridge University Press, 1990, pp. xviii, 280. A study of the different types of institutionalized arrangements for administrating small scale common property resources.

Ostrom, Vincent. *The Intellectual Crisis in American Public Administration.* (The University of Alabama Press) 1973, pp. 74-133. Ostrom investigates and discusses the structure of a democratic administration which would be based on overlapping jurisdictions and fragmented authority. This model is presented as a challenge, a new paradigm, to the old paradigm of bureaucratic public administration.

Palda, Filip, ed. *Provincial Trade Wars: Why the Blockade Must End.* Vancouver: The Fraser Institute, 1994. This book details the high cost imposed on Canadians by interprovincial trade barriers and explains why Canadians can no longer ignore these costs.

Tullock, Gordon. *Private Wants, Public Means: An Economic Analysis of the Desirable Scope of Government.* New York: Basic

Books, Inc., 1970, pp. 3-28 and 71-95. The collective decision-making problem is analyzed by use of an example,
mosquito abatement. The issues of individual costs, free
riding, and provision are answered within the context of
the analysis. The economics of externalities create uncer-
tainty and additional activities for government, since collective decision-making does not always deal efficiently
with externalities.

Tiebout, Charles M. "An Economic Theory of Fiscal Decentralization" *Public Finances: Needs, Sources, and Utilization*. National Bureau of Economic Research, Princeton: Princeton
University Press, 1961.

Tiebout, Charles M. "Location Theory, Empirical Evidence and
Economic Evolution," *Papers and Proceedings of the Regional
Science Association*, 3 (1957) pp. 75-82. Two basic papers on
the "Tiebout" effect.

Tullock, Gordon. *Wealth, Poverty and Politics*. (New York: Basil
Blackwell) 1988, pp. 8-43. The form of a decision-making
process will influence policy outcomes. In a democracy,
voting is part of the decision-making process, so it will
ultimately effect policy.

Whalley, John. "Induced Distortions of Interprovincial Activity:
An Overview of the Issues." In *Federalism and the Canadian
Economic Union*. Edited by Michael J. Trebilcock et al. Toronto: Ontario Economic Council, 1983. An overview of
how Canadian provincial governments install barriers to
the movement of goods and people within the country.

Chapter 4: "Sociological" Federalism as a Way of Reducing Ethnic and Religious Tension

Parallel governments

IT SHOULD BE EMPHASIZED that subordinate governments do not have to have geographic monopolies. In the United States we frequently find that the school board is a separate governmental unit with its own elected board. It sometimes does and sometimes does not have the same geographic boundaries as the local government. In Tucson, for example, the city and most of its suburbs elect a board for the Tucson Unified School District. There is no other government unit with exactly the same borders, but about 2/3 of the voters in the school board election also vote in Tucson municipal elections. People who live in the suburbs vote for their own local governments which deal with non-school matters.[16]

---

16   A couple of small suburbs have their own independent school systems.

There's nothing particularly surprising about this. I simply give it as an example of the point that it is not essential that all government units in any given geographic area be hierarchically arranged.

Actually, in the area around most American cities, a great many rather special governmental agencies will be found. The water and sewer system frequently is, as in the case of Tucson, operated by an "authority" which is specially provided by legislation in the state and whose members are appointed by the various different local governments or by the governor of the state. In some cases they are elected, although that is rare. Canada is moving in the same direction, as an increasing number of special agencies and joint boards are being created to provide services for groups and municipalities. Since 1981 in Quebec regional councils have been formed with responsibilities for defining land use, making property assessments, and operating waste management systems.

The basic objective in democratic government is to have the government behave as much as possible in accordance with the wishes of its citizens. Unfortunately this frequently means only with the wishes of a majority. One of the real problems is the citizens' lack of strong motives, in large government bodies, to become well informed and hence supervise the government efficiently. As a complication, having too many government agencies in and of itself causes difficulties for the functioning of the system. But if the citizen can only vote intelligently for, say, five governments, they do not have to be all hierarchical, with one above the other. They can be parallel, as the Tucson School Board and city government are.

Current and historical examples

Parallel government is not in any way a radical suggestion, although the language that I am using to discuss it is quite different from what is customary. It may be that one of the reasons that a number of parallel governments is normally not thought of as a set of separate governments is that in the United States all governments below the level of the state are "creatures of the state." This means that legally and constitutionally the state can organize or reorganize them more or less as it wishes. Similarly in Canada the Constitution Act of 1867 makes local government the responsibility of the provincial legislatures.

Since the state has single-member districts, it is a collection of geographically elected officials, so it normally does not do anything which the populace of a local area would find highly objectionable. It is nevertheless true that it can, whenever it wishes, shift the local governments around.[17] The communes in Switzerland are somewhat more secure in their relations with the cantons.

History tells us that the whole of Western Europe during much of the period from the fall of Rome until very modern times was subject to two separate governments. There were the feudal lords and there was the church. Although they did not always get along very well there was nevertheless a division of labour. In spite of periodic challenges, most matters having to do with family relations, divorce,[18] education, and a number of other areas were matters for the church. Of course, towards the end of

---

17   As a matter of practical fact, this is normally done by those members of the state legislature who are elected from the particular part of the state that the changes are suggested for. As a rough rule of thumb, the Arizona state legislature will do anything in the way of reorganizing Pima County that is desired by all of the members of the two houses that come from Pima County and will do nothing objected to by all of them. If they are split, the odds are quite good that the state will decide to do nothing, but it might possibly opt in favour of the majority of the local representatives.

18   Strictly speaking banned, but actually influential noblemen could separate by pretending that the marriage was invalid from the beginning.

this period there were a good many bishops who were also feudal lords.

The situation in a way continued in the English-speaking world until very recently, and ceremonially to the present. There were two court systems, one of which was the so-called common law system and the other of which was equity. Equity was originally part of the church with a clerical official at its top. Eventually, the Lord Chancellor of England ceased to be clerically trained and became a man who had been trained in the separate law of equity.

The basic objective in democratic government
is to have the government behave
as much as possible in accordance
with the wishes of its citizens.

This system was transferred to most of North America and in fact we had two sets of courts—one equity and one common law—until well into the 19th century. What then happened was that the courts were combined in the specific sense that the same person who was a common law judge would become a Chancellor in equity if the case was the sort that required equity rather than common law. Today the merger has gone further, but there still are two separate branches of the law even if the judge no longer announces that he has ceased to be a judge to become a chancellor. The province of Quebec is unique in North America in that it does not operate under common law but under *le droit civil* which has its roots in the legal reforms of the Roman emperor Justinian and the French ruler Napoleon. In practice however the Civil Code of Quebec operates much like the common law.

Following the ancient Turks

The point of the preceding examples is to make it clear that we can have parallel governments as well as vertically separated ones. This is very convenient for many things—in particular, areas where technical considerations make it convenient to have separate authorities.

In this chapter I suggest another way of setting up parallel governments which is actually lifted not from the democratic culture of the Canada, the United States or Switzerland, but from the despotic system of the ancient Turks. The inhabitant of the old Turkish Empire was, for many purposes, subject to the local governor appointed by the Padishah. In a number of other areas, however, the citizen was subject to a parallel government organized by his church. Of course, if he was a good member of the Islamic community, the two governments would be more or less identical.

The system is not confined to despotic countries, however. Between the wars Estonia had an almost exact analogy which was basically democratic. Czechoslovakia and Hungary, indeed all of the former Austro-Hungarian Empire, had rather weaker but similar systems. Canada and the United States have no similar system as a matter of strict law, but we are countries of immigrants. In most of our larger cities a recently arrived Lithuanian will find that most of his dealings with the city government can be with co-ethnics who hold city jobs.

We tend to think of Athens as the foundation of our democracy and interestingly they had a similar institution. Their law code provided:

> If a deme or phrateres or worshippers of heroes or gennetai or drinking groups or funerary clubs or religious guilds or pirates [*sic!*] or traders make rules amongst

themselves, these shall be valid unless they are in conflict with public law.[19]

Clearly, this was permitting a great many special voluntary organizations with parallel powers to those of the regular government. The existence of such organizations can even today give individuals greater ability to control government institutions under which they live and to defuse certain types of tension which might otherwise exist. The latter is particularly difficult in areas where people of radically different customs and traditions are deeply intermingled.[20]

Although this system is particularly helpful when you have a mix of different people from different traditions and language backgrounds, it can also work when the population is quite homogeneous provided only that that population contains groups that differ from the others in any one of many ways.

Nuts and bolts of parallel government

Let us discuss briefly how parallel government could work. Let us suppose that the central government, in addition to laying out various geographic subdivisions, also provides "associations" that have jurisdictions of a non-geographic nature. They deal, say, with intrafamily relations and education of the children. They would of necessity have to have tax authority over their members, but since their members would enter completely voluntarily there is no reason to worry about that.

---

19   Oswyn Murray, "Life and Society in Classical Greece," *Greece and the Hellenistic World*, Oxford History of the Classical World, edited by John Boardman, Jasper Griffin, and Oswyn Murray, (Oxford, 1988), p. 203.

20   See my "A New Proposal for Decentralizing Government Activity," *Rationale Wirtschaftspolitik In Komplexen Gesellschaften*, Helmuth Milde und Hans G. Monissen (Hrsg), Grard Gfgen, Stuttgart, 1985, pp 139-48.

Much of the population might not be interested in becoming a member of one of these associations. If that were true, the state would maintain a fallback educational system, divorce court, etc. Thus, only people who positively wanted to would be members of these associations. It would probably also be necessary to put certain restraints on what the associations could do since they could generate externalities by sufficiently outrageous behaviour. But if we follow the Athenian model, any rules they make are valid unless they violate laws in the larger society, for instance against murder.

We already have many examples of overlapping rule systems. Throughout the civilized world today dispute resolution is normally available from non-legal sources. It is called arbitration in English and various other terms in other nations, and a great deal of use is made of it. In general, the arbitral tribunal, whatever it is, reaches a decision but does not have the organs of coercion—the sheriff, police, army, etc.—to enforce its decisions.

If the person who has lost out in the litigation before an arbitral tribunal does not want to obey the decision, the winner must go to a regular court for appropriate court orders which will be enforced by the police. As a normal rule, this is a very simple matter, but it does provide a check on the possibility of rules which are contrary to public policy.

And if the associations for which I am arguing existed, there would also be no particular reason why they could not make arrangements among themselves for dealing with disputes which ran across different associations. Supposing that I, having become a good Roman Catholic, and being a member of an association of which the Bishop is the local authority, have an auto accident with an Orthodox Jew who is a member of another association. If the Roman Catholic Church and the Orthodox Jewish Church had an agreement for this matter, there is no reason that it could not be referred to some kind of combined dispute resolution procedure.

Education and parallel government

The advantage of this particular type of federalization, or decentralization, is that it provides for greater individual choice as to the type of government to which one is subject. Such organizations are ideally suited to government activities in which there are no economies of scale. Education is a prime example. Substantially no economy of scale is involved in education unless you happen to live in a lightly populated area. Thus, permitting the existence of several school systems is not in any way impossible or even problematic. Indeed, most countries do permit it.

In most Western countries, the rule that students go to designated public schools has been strongly enforced, although there seems to be no explanation for this other than custom. As a matter of fact, at the moment, this particular system seems to be on the verge of breaking down. "Choice in education" is a major slogan in the U.S. and in the Canadian province of Alberta, and there is no reason to believe that at the practical level it will cause difficulties.

Education and voter preferences would be well served if it were possible for the individual associations to tax their members for education and the general government would tax, for educational purposes, only those citizens who are not members of an association that provides education. Personally, I would not have any particular objection to associations which didn't provide education but it would not be possible to excuse people from those associations' school taxes when they joined them.

Marriage

There are many other areas where there is no great difficulty in running independent associations rather than a central government. There doesn't seem to be very much in the way of rational justification for the various legal arrangements for family relations. Different countries have radically different arrangements and in the Canada and the United States traditional arrangements are breaking down. The result is that people have quite different marital arrangements, but there's only one set of courts and one set of laws.

An Arab prince who arrives in New York with four wives and three concubines is not going to be bothered by the police. But in the event he does get into legal difficulties with his wives and concubines, he will face a legal system which really is not suitable. Semi-contractual arrangements are replacing regular marriages. In this area, too, the existing law is quite inappropriate.

Of course we do not necessarily feel that just anything can be done in the way of marital arrangements. In the town of Bountiful in the province of British Columbia the Mormon practice of polygamy recently came under criticism. The practice is illegal in Canada but for the most part a blind eye has been turned to it. However, allegations of brainwashing and forced marriages in Bountiful have stirred some public opposition. This is reminiscent of 19th century America, when one of the great problems that the Mormons faced was their custom of plural marriages; indeed they gave up the custom in order to become an integral part of the United States. Isolated incidents in Bountiful B.C. notwithstanding, I suspect few would care today.

In any event, this is another area where clearly there is no need for the government to have a monopoly. No doubt there would have to be some kind of fallback law for people who did not join one of the associations, or for people who are in an association which did not provide a full budget of services. But that is not a great problem.

Moving between governments

Having various governments defined sociologically instead of geographically should permit individuals greater freedom in the sense that they will have mainly people who agree with each other in each of these sociological organizations. Further, voting with their feet would be particularly easy in this case. It would not be necessary to move, only to change your registration.

Of course, people changing registration from one of these associations to another would have to fulfil their obligations to the old association before they moved. We could not permit people to switch from Association A to Association B if the switch occurred the day before the taxes of Association A were to be collected and the day after the taxes of Association B were collected. Once again this is not a significant problem. It requires specific arrangements but not difficult ones.

Problems with parallel government

There are two problems which are raised by any division of government into parts, whether geographical or, as in this chapter, sociological. One of these problems is simply the likelihood of internal wars. The other is the fact that the various divisions, whether geographical or sociological, are likely to have different levels of wealth, and many people think that equalizing wealth is one of the major functions of government. Both these problems are probably more important with geographical than with sociological divisions. Both are also more important with the divisions between nations than with internal divisions within a nation.

Fighting between different ethnic groups is historically very common inside almost all countries that have more than one such group. In general, it can be kept down to a relatively low level because there will be other government groups or organizations with considerable force at their disposal that object to such rioting. The kind of sociological federalization we are now discussing might well, in and of itself, reduce the amount of such rioting. A great many causes of dispute, such as school curriculums, would vanish if the schools simply adjusted their courses to the various sociological groups.

Unfortunately, not all. The various views on whether or not women can have an abortion are not easily dealt with. Anti-abortionists feel that abortion is murder and should be prevented no matter who is having it or what her religion is. On the other hand, the pro-abortionists feel not only that they have a right to have an abortion, but that the government should pay for it in some circumstances. This particular bit of tension is not likely to be dealt with by the kind of sociological federalism I am discussing.

Having various governments defined
sociologically instead of geographically
should permit individuals greater freedom
in the sense that they will have mainly people
who agree with each other in each of these
sociological organizations.

If we consider income redistribution, it is fairly obvious that a number of religious groups do a much better job taking care of the poor within them—and for that matter making gifts for the poor who are not within them—than governments do. The Mormons, for example, don't like to see their members on relief and have procedures for impoverished communicants in their church. There is no doubt that these work much better than the government programs.

The basic difficulty that people raise with respect to this area, however, is not internal transfers but instead the problem of different sociological or geographic areas having different levels of wealth.

The basic rule here is, as far as possible, to make use of the local governments or the sociological governments for the actual distribution of the funds. Nevertheless, there should be some kind of arrangement so that transfers are made from the wealthier areas or groups to the poorer ones.

Conclusion

As far as I know, the suggestion for sociological federalism has not been canvassed anywhere in the western countries. On the other hand, things that rather resemble it have existed in western countries even if they're not talked about in this way. For many countries this particular type of governmental decentralization would have additional advantages which make it highly desirable. This is particularly true in those cases in which different ethnic groups are geographically intertwined.

Bibliography

Aun, Karl. "On the Spirit of the Estonian Minorities Law," *Excerptum Apophoreta Tartuensia*. Stockholm: Societas Litterarium Estonica in Svecio, 1949.

Aun, Karl. "Cultural Autonomy of Ethnic Minorities in Estonia: A Model for Multicultural Society." Paper presented at 3rd Conference of Baltic Studies in Scandinavia in Stockholm, June 1975.

Aun, Karl. "The Cultural Autonomy of National Minorities in Estonia." *Yearbook of the Estonian Learned Society in America* I, 1951-1953. These three papers provide an excellent example of "sociological federalism." The papers provide a history of the establishment of legislation which allowed minorities in Estonia to form autonomous cultural units and outlines the structures of these autonomous units.

Tullock, Gordon. "A New Proposal for Decentralizing Government Activity" in *Rational Wirtschaftspolitik in Komplexen Gesellschaften*, edited by Hellmuth Milde and Hans G. Monissen. Stutgart: Verlag W. Kohlhammer GmBH, 1985 (article in English), pp. 139-148. A somewhat more formal presentation of the argument of this chapter.

Chapter 5:
Democracy As It Really Is

The least imperfect system

UP UNTIL NOW WE HAVE SIMPLY assumed that the government will be democratic and have said relatively little about how democracy works. It is now time to repair the omission.

Democracy, like other human institutions, is not perfect. Indeed, it is decidedly imperfect. Winston Churchill once said that "Democracy is the worst of forms of government except, of course, for those others that have been tried from time to time." This chapter will tell you a number of things about democracy that may disillusion some enthusiasts. They should keep in mind that although democracy is far from perfect, the other forms of government are generally much worse.

A point to be kept in mind is that democracy at its best carries out the will of some of the people. The problem with this is that the people are generally not very well informed, have not thought very much about what is going on, and may be completely ignorant of what most intellectuals would think of as rather basic facts. Intellectuals frequently are quite annoyed by the decisions taken by democracies. Intellectuals tend to be attracted by powerful myths and the totalitarian systems generate such things. The common man or woman tends to be more sceptical. That is not because they are better informed but simply because they are less easily influenced. They are as likely to be sceptical about a new and true idea as about a new and false idea.

The role and behaviour of elected officials

Let us begin by looking at the other end of the democratic government, the elected officials. The first thing to be said about this is that there is a very considerable difference between the elected officials of large central governments and the elected officials of small organizations like my Sunshine Mountain Homeowners' Association. The first group are obviously people who are in the business of making a living by winning elections. The second group are made up of people who, in a way, are pursuing their hobbies.

Consequences of vote maximizing

The fact that the high or low official has to get elected or, in the case of civil service, has to deal with superiors who are elected, has distinct effects on their behaviour: to survive in office they will have to maximize votes.

The politician who has carefully studied the problem is more informed than the average voter. This informed politician might develop a platform which does not simply reflect the preferences of his or her constituents precisely because it *does* reflect their interests, which they do not fully understand. Such a platform does not maximize votes. And the politician who behaves contrary to the wishes of the voter might be an admirable person but he or she would not be carrying out the "will of the people." The fact that the average voter is not well informed, may have very narrow interests, has only average intelligence, etc. means that most of us frequently feel that the decisions produced by these "maximizing politicians" are depressing.

Vote trading and voter ignorance

A politician, if he is a good politician, does not simply find out what a majority of his constituents want and then do it. He is aware of the fact that people not only have views on various issues but that these views vary in intensity from one person to another. A great many of the voters might not even find out how the politician voted on many issues or if they do find out, will forget about it by the time of the next election. This combination of ignorance and differing intensity of desire allows what is know as "vote trading" or "logrolling." An example can best be used to describe and understand this phenomenon.

> *. . . democracy at its best carries out the will of some of the people. The problem with this is that the people are generally not very well informed, have not thought very much about what is going on, and may be completely ignorant of what most intellectuals would think of as rather basic facts.*

Large amounts of money are spent subsidizing rather prosperous farmers. Further, food is made more expensive and the gain to the farmers is much less than the social costs. How do these things get through? After all, only a minority of all congressmen represent farm districts. The vast bulk of Congress represents people whose only concern with this matter is that they will end up paying higher taxes and food prices.

The answer is a combination of trades and voter ignorance. Let us begin with the trades. Agriculture is a particularly good example because we recently had an effort by Congressman Armey, a former professor of economics, at least to restrict the agricultural subsidy and price-raising conspiracy run by the federal government. He offered in the House an amendment to the agricultural program providing that no one whose income from non-farming activities exceeded $125,000 a year was to receive any subsidy.

One would think that Congressman Armey's amendment would have been bottled up in committee, but he is a clever congressman and succeeded in avoiding that trap. Once it had appeared on the floor, you would think that practically no congressman would be willing to vote openly against it. As a matter of fact, he was beaten by 2-1 on a recorded vote.

Armey's own comment about all of this was revealing: "There are no weak sisters on the agricultural committee—they do what committees do very well. They spend five years filling their silos with chits and then they call them in." What happened was simple. Individual members of the agricultural committee had cast votes for various things that benefitted other special interests. In return, when the farm issue came up, the congressmen for whom they had done these previous favours paid off by voting for the agricultural program.

A great many European governments, although they operate in just exactly the way I have described above, do so in a rather covert way so it is not obvious. Vote trading is also less obvious in Canada where very strong party discipline precludes Members of Parliament from voting against their party. However there are issues on which all parties vote together, and laws are often modified at the committee stage to reflect the concerns of opposition parties. The process of bargaining is simply less obvious in Canada than in the U.S.

Is vote trading undesirable? First, consider the simple argument in favour of vote trading: suppose that I want A and object to B but my feelings with respect to A are much stronger than those with respect to B. I find someone else who wants B and objects to A but whose feelings are much stronger with respect to B than to A. If we now agree to have both A and B, both of us would be better off than if we didn't have either A or B. Intensity of preference should be taken into account in voting as well as simple direction of preference.

This is so obvious that it is surprising it is not discussed more frequently. If one looks over the vast mass of legislation passed by Congress each session, it is fairly obvious that most of us would be indifferent to most of it. By this I do not mean that we are indifferent to the whole Department of Defense budget but that we are indifferent with respect to such issues as which particular air base shall be opened or closed.

There are, however, two problems with this favourable view of vote trading, the first of which is that after all you only have to get a majority in order to get a bill through. This means that the bargain must benefit only a majority of constituencies and can injure the country as a whole. Suppose, for example, we have some collection of special interest measures which benefit 218 (a majority) congressmen's constituencies by $1,500 apiece, but which impose a tax of $1,000 on each of the 435 constituencies in the United States. There is thus a tax of $435,000, and benefits of $327,000. The benefit is less than the cost.

Of course, such cases are marginal, but nevertheless they can occur even if everyone is perfectly informed. Granted that people are far from perfectly informed, however, this kind of thing can become much more serious. It is probably true that most citizens are reasonably well informed about measures that are directly aimed at their particular small special interest, but pretty much uninformed about other matters. This is not a criticism or even a statement that they are irrational. It costs time and energy to become well informed. Being better informed about things that directly concern you than about things that are only peripheral is a sensible economy.

The result of this, however, is that bills can be, and are, passed in which the cost is very, very much greater, spread thin across the country as a whole, than the benefit to the small special interest group that does benefit. The Central Arizona Project (CAP), at immense cost to the taxpayers of the United States, will provide water to certain parts of Arizona at a very, very heavily subsidized price. Although the total cost to the citizens of the United States is very great, the cost, if divided out citizen by citizen, is low. The benefit to people living in certain parts of Arizona, however, is highly concentrated and hence this was a politically paying activity. Canada is no stranger either to the perverse consequences of concentrated benefits and dissipated costs. Phone companies, textile mills, dairy farmers, and a host of other producers survive on government granted monopoly rights, at the expense of consumers. These consumers grumble, but the extra few cents they pay per quart of milk or for a phone call gives them little incentive to protest on Parliament Hill or lobby their representatives. The humble consumer sits on the sidelines as politicians balance the different intensities of special interest group feelings.

This is probably the reason that the average citizen is shown regularly in public opinion polls as disliking his legislature, which he realizes puts a heavy tax burden on him, but being very strongly in favour of his own representative who he realizes gets him various special privileges. It is presumably true that in a vague way the citizen knows that his representative is making these bargains and probably that the bargains on the whole are not to his advantage. He also knows, however, that if his representative, alone of all the representatives, refused to enter into these bargains, he would be much worse off than he is. He assumes that the representative is making a good thing out of a basically bad institutional structure. And as a matter of fact, in most cases he is quite right.

Small government limits vote trading

One of the advantages of decentralizing the government, or what we call "federalism," is that it does indeed make these bargains somewhat more restricted. The relatively restricted geographic scope of the bargains that can be made makes it more likely that the voters will know about those bargains which inconvenience them, even if only slightly, than they will in a massive government area.

Conclusion

All of us are members of the Great Society or the Just Society, but also the members of very many smaller groups. Getting the government to do things important to the Society's interests and in accord with those of the small groups is desirable. Unfortunately, these are sometimes in conflict and also it is very commonly true that the interests of one small group are in conflict with those of another. This chapter has tried to set out these conflicts and explain how they can be resolved, at least partially.

The federal system does not eliminate every clash, but it does reduce the total number. At the same time, it changes their nature somewhat. Problems between different branches of the government become more common and squabbles between bureaucracies in the same government or between different groups of citizens within a jurisdiction become less common. On the whole, there is a net gain from federalism.

Once again, the main theme of this book up to this point has been that democracy is better than other forms of government and that a federal democracy with a good deal of decentralization is better than a centralized democracy. I emphasize, however, that this does not mean that either of these forms of government are perfect. There are defects to all human institutions, including federal democracy.

Bibliography

Olson, Mancur. *The Logic of Collective Action: Public Goods and the Theory of Groups.* Cambridge: Harvard University Press, 1965, pp. 111-167. When written, this was a major contribution. Now it is the orthodox theory of pressure groups and a treatment of the dynamics of special interest groups.

Rowley, Charles K., Tollison, Robert D., and Tullock, Gordon ed. *The Political Economy of Rent-Seeking.* Boston: Kluwer, 1988. A compendium of recent work on pressure groups.

Chapter 6:
A Bouquet of Governments

THE PURPOSE OF THIS CHAPTER is to describe simply and critique briefly the very wide diversity of different kinds of democratic institutions that have been used both in federal and non-federal states. Diversity is greater among federal countries than among non-federal, but it's quite significant among unitary states as well.

What is "necessary" government service?

The existing diversity among governments is great enough so that many things most people think are inevitable are by no means universal. To take one example, sewage disposal is usually regarded as an activity which requires a good deal of centralization because of the economies of scale. In other words, it's much cheaper for the city of Tucson and its suburbs to all have one sewage disposal plant than it would be to have a set of small ones.

Water is another example which is normally thought to require centralization. On one occasion I visited a rather posh suburb of Athens in Greece and discovered, to my surprise, that the water there was provided privately by tank trucks. Each house had a cistern and they bought water as they needed it from various private water companies.

This had one unusual convenience. Water was available in several different qualities and prices. If you were going to be away from your home and simply wanted to keep the lawn watered, you bought cheap water, but if you were going to be there and expected to drink it you bought the high quality.[21] Once again, I have no idea whether this is more or less efficient than providing water by a centralized pipe system, but certainly the people in the suburb did not seem to be annoyed by it.

These two examples have been given as an indication that many things which we tend to think of as necessary activities in government may not be. In other words, careful thought should be given to each activity. Needless to say, it is easier to give thought to local problems if you have a federal state than if you have a unitary one.

What is the "best" way to run government?

Now let us turn to actual governmental organizations. I should like to start discussing very small local governments such as the one that runs my Sunshine Mountain Ridge Homeowners' Association. The first thing to be said is that the members of the governing council are not paid. We have no judiciary, although the council or its members on occasion might perform functions which are somewhat like that of a judiciary. They may deal with a quarrel between two members of the association by listening to both of them and then making a decision. Our little government also has important diplomatic functions. Dealing with the higher

---

21   Tucson has a rule which is rather similar. Golf courses are required to water their fairways with second hand water from the sewage disposal plant. It sometimes smells.

level of governments and with neighbouring local governments is one of its more important activities. This description of the local government would fit very many small farming villages.

As we move to larger governments with greater responsibilities, the level of formal structure grows. One example is that usually the legislators and higher executives of national governments receive a salary. But although this is usual, it is not by any means universal. The Swiss legislature receives no pay, although there is a rather generous expense account.

. . . many things which we tend to think of as necessary activities in government may not be. In other words, careful thought should be given to each activity.

This of course raises the questions of whether we want the legislators to be true professionals, i.e. people who make their living as legislators, or whether we want them to be amateurs, people whose primary role in life is something else and who are willing to devote part of their time to being a legislator. There are arguments for both of these positions.

The professional legislator would presumably be better informed about legislative business than the, let us say, lawyer who spends six weeks every two years (officially this is what is supposed to be done in Virginia) as a legislator. On the other hand, such a legislator is not as good a representative of the average person as one who is himself closer to the average.

There is another aspect to this, which is that amateur legislators are apt to spend very much less time legislating. In other words, the total number of laws passed is apt to be much smaller and their length is apt to be shorter.[22] Of course under present circumstances, with national legislatures passing very long bills that no member has actually read in full, this characteristic may not be very important.

However, some form of voluntarism still exists at this higher level of government. Voluntary boards are to be found throughout democratic governments. Indeed, they are frequently found in dictatorships as well. They may be temporary, appointed to consider a given problem, or permanent, like the board of a university. In both cases they bring prominent citizens who are not formally members of the government into a decision-making role. In some cases they are brought in to avoid decisions. Politicians sometimes appoint a commission to investigate some problem for the sole specific purpose of delaying a decision. The British and more recently the Canadians have made an art of this procedure.

[Do] we want the legislators to be true professionals, i.e. people who make their living as legislators, or . . . [do] we want them to be amateurs, people whose primary role in life is something else and who are willing to devote part of their time to being a legislator?

There is another example of individual citizens who make quite important decisions in Anglo-Saxon countries and some other democracies. These are the jurymen. This is a form of conscription, in which the average citizen is called upon occasionally (selected by lot) to serve on a small board to determine the

---

22   "No man's property is safe: the legislature is in session." Normally attributed to Mencken.

outcome of criminal prosecutions and lawsuits. In the United States, more than in Canada or perhaps any other country, it is probable that this particular democratic institution makes more decisions in an average year than all of the other democratic institutions put together. Of course these are particular detailed decisions, but nevertheless they are quite important.[23]

It should be said with respect to all of these groups of private citizens that they are normally neither very well informed about the subject matter that they are dealing with nor deeply impressed with the existing law. Juries in particular are well known to follow their conscience rather than the law when the two are in conflict.[24] Whether this is an advantage or a disadvantage is not obvious.

Moving to larger governments—county, city, etc.—the first thing we note is that there is often a distinction between the legislature and the executive. One of the explanations for this is that as the government gets larger the number of total decisions made grows and there is much to be said for allocating a lot of the less important decisions to permanent, non-elected officials. Of course, in many cases there is a sort of mix. In Canada and in the cabinets of most European governments are elected members of the legislature and in many cities, like Tucson for example, the

---

23   In order to be candid with the reader, I should say that I do not like the jury. See my *Trials on Trial*, Columbia University Press, New York, 1980.

24   According to the *New York Times*, May 5, 1991, p. A11, a poor Hispanic immigrant had a sick three year old. He and his wife took her in their car to get some medicine. Since the child was feverish and crying, her mother held her, rather than strapping her into a safety seat as required by an enforced law. There was an accident and the child was killed. The father was charged with murder. The prospect that a jury would convict in such a case is so small that I suspect the prosecutor could stand psychiatric help. The judge, who retained his sanity, dismissed the case without bothering a jury. (*New York Times*, May 6, p. A1.)

mayor is both the chief executive and a voting member of the city council. Indeed, he presides over the city council.

Large government must "contract out"

In larger governments, however, more formal arrangements for performing their various activities will normally be made. We begin by an extreme example, the Lakewood Plan.

Lakewood is a suburb of Los Angeles with a population of about 80,000 who decided some time ago that they really did not need to have many employees. Specifically, their government consisted of the city council, an engineer who negotiated contracts with suppliers of governmental services, and one secretary. They obtained all the other government services by contract, mainly with other government agencies in the immediate vicinity. For example, they got their police by contract with the Los Angeles County Sheriff's Department, the city of Los Angeles undertook to collect their taxes, the streets were cleaned by private contractors, and so on. The system was quite successful and a number of other cities in that area have copied it more or less. But Lakewood itself has recently switched to doing some of the activities itself.

All over the United States there are lots of experiments by local government in contracting things out instead of maintaining their own staff. I have mentioned before that if my house catches on fire the fire extinguishing will be done by Rural Metro, a private company. The local van service for the handicapped is contracted out by the city. The difference between contracting out and hiring your own personnel is not quite as severe as it might appear. In both cases, people are hired to do the job. The difference is whether they are hired in collective groups by way of a contract, let us say the Los Angeles Sheriff's Department, or individually.

In Canada there has been less experimenting with contracting out and this may be related to a trend away from local government responsibility. The provincial governments have in recent years come to exert a greater control over municipalities. The provinces have encouraged small local administrations to amalgamate, and many services that were once provided at the community level are now provided by regional administrative boards.

Job security and government efficiency

The basic point of this discussion is that there are many different ways of running a government. There is, however, something to be said about the efficiency of the various ways. The first thing to be said is that employment security is undesirable if you want to get the work done. Waste collection in the area around Tucson is contracted out. Sometimes there are shifts from one contractor to another, which means that we get better prices and service than we would if we entered into a 30-year contract.

> *. . . as the government gets larger the number of total decisions made grows and there is much to be said for allocating a lot of the less important decisions to permanent, non-elected officials.*

One of the reasons we get better service is that the companies we deal with do not have 30-year contracts with their employees. Most modern governments have adopted various civil service arrangements which involve more or less lifetime employment unless the employee voluntarily quits. This normally leads to much less efficient performance of the government's business than it would get if it had more normal employment relations with its employees.

The civil servants, then, are a powerful political group who become more powerful as their numbers increase and who push very heavily for their own interests. It is to all intents and purposes impossible to fire an American Federal Government civil servant unless he decides not to fight.[25]

In practice, I do not think it makes a great deal of difference whether you hire your employees in the executive branch individually or by groups through contracting. What does make a difference is ensuring that they not have permanent tenure. This, of course, is directly contrary to the conventional wisdom.[26] The present situation in many governments is that the elected officials and those higher ranking officials whom they are permitted to appoint at will cannot fire lower level officials if the lower level officials do not do as they are instructed.

On the other hand, the lower level officials, by way of carefully calculated leaks to the press or possibly in some cases

---

25 The *New York Times*, Friday, May 3, 1991, pages 1-13, LA edition, carried a story about a serious problem in the New York City Civil Service. New York has a very large welfare program and as part of this program it maintains a large warehouse in which various supplies for the administrators of the program or things to be distributed to the poor are kept. For many years the staff of this warehouse have been engaged in systematic large scale theft, sometimes driving things away by the truckload. Mr. Fourey, in the city's Department of Investigations, found out about this and began investigations and submitted a great many memos to his superiors demanding that some action be taken to stop it. The result was that during an economy drive he was fired. The *New York Times*, in a long story, shows great indignation about all of this, but notably does not suggest that the civil servants running the warehouse be fired. Indeed, it would probably be much easier to convict them of crimes and imprison them than it would be to discharge them.

26 Conventional wisdom also frequently maintains that civil servants can be fired if they are inefficient. Most of the people who say this haven't tried.

deliberate disobedience to orders, can generate very bad publicity for their political superiors. This may well lead to the dismissal of the higher level, political, appointees. Under the circumstances, the higher officials are normally unwilling to grab the bull by the horns and attempt to force their permanent civil servants into efficiency. If they could fire them, or if the inferiors were employees of a corporation which could lose its contract, they would have much more control.

The problem is exacerbated by the fact that most civil servants positions are either over- or under-paid. Civil service rates are determined by elaborate committees that allegedly set them at their private equivalents. Of course, it is not obvious what the private equivalent of any given government job is. We frequently observe long queues of people trying to take some government jobs. On the other hand, other government jobs are impossible to fill unless you are willing to accept very poor quality people. It would appear that these pay scales are badly out of equilibrium. There are far more people who want to work for the Post Office than are needed. They are also paid more than their much more efficient private enterprise equivalents in Federal Express, Purolator, etc. On the other hand I have observed two state-run universities in which the salaries for secretaries are low enough that qualified secretaries cannot be hired under that title.

The above remarks will be regarded by many as such a severe deviation from the norm as to be actually sinful. The view that we need civil service is very widely held. I would encourage governments who do not already have one to avoid falling into this trap. The civil servants will rapidly organize themselves into a pressure group and once they've done it, democratic government has very great difficulty in dealing with them. An indication of the power of this group comes from surveys which show that in Canada, a country with a vast and well entrenched civil service, interest groups devote 40 percent of their lobbying efforts to bureaucrats. In the U.S. the figure is closer to 20 percent.

The executive and political branches

The radical distinction between the executive and the political branch is frequently much less obvious in smaller government units. In the American system, the Chief Executive is normally directly elected. In Canada and in most European democracies that person is chosen by the lower house of the legislature. The result is that in the United States, the Chief Executive is frequently of opposite party from the majority of the legislature. As American Chief Executives have veto power over legislation, this means that in a way they serve as a third house of the legislature. Their veto can normally be overruled only by a reinforced majority of both houses.

This problem (or advantage, as the case may be), does not arise in Parliamentary systems where the Prime Minister depends throughout his tenure on maintaining support of a majority of the legislature. In two or three party systems this is fairly easy, but in multi-party systems keeping the coalition together may be quite complex. France is experimenting with a sort of combination.

Many American state governments have officials in the executive branch who are elected, not appointed, by the governor. One very common example is the chief fiscal officer, who is frequently separately elected. This seems to me a very sensible institution, since one of the purposes of the chief fiscal officer is to check on expenditures, and having an independent official there is sensible.

Most levels of U.S. governments have converged on the Canadian practice of appointing most executive positions. The state of Arizona has only a few executive officers, mainly holding not very important positions, who are directly elected. The holder of one of these minor and unimportant offices, the secretary of state, suddenly became the governor of the state about two years ago as a result of an impeachment of the elected governor. She served efficiently and well but apparently decided that she would do badly in the upcoming election and therefore did not run. She has been replaced by a directly elected governor.

The veto

The American institution of the executive veto perhaps deserves some comment. It exists in three forms. The first of these is the one in which original Constitution permits the President to veto any congressional bill as a whole. Congress has the right to overturn his veto by two-thirds majority of both houses.

The second form permits the governor of many states (the President now wants this power) to go through a bill and veto specific clauses in it. This is primarily thought of for budgetary provisions and is called the line item veto. Once again, it can be overturned by two-thirds majority in both houses, although the exact rule varies from state to state.

The third form permits the governor, and once again the President would like this power, to reduce a given appropriation item rather than abolishing it. He might make it only 90 percent of what the legislature has passed. Although it looks minor, it is actually the strongest form, because it is much harder to get a two-thirds majority, or even a simple majority, to overturn a small reduction in a budget item than to overturn the actual abolition of some particular expenditure.

Whether the veto is a good idea or not depends on a lot of general philosophical considerations. It is more or less useless if you have a cabinet form of government. If the Prime Minister is in fact selected by the legislature then this whole process would have no purpose. The veto for a separately elected executive, whether the President or governor or for that matter the mayor, is an excellent idea because an executive elected by the entire body of the voters is somewhat less subservient to local pressure groups than are the legislators who individually are elected by only a part of the electorate. A majority of the voters in a majority of the legislative constituencies can be only a little more than 25 percent of the voters. They might get something through the legislature, but it would be harder to avoid the presidential veto.

Relationships between governments

Let us now consider the relationship among governments. The first thing to be said is that if you go to a Canadian, American or Swiss city, you find a dense web of additional government organizations performing all sorts of functions. It may be park boards dealing with parks scattered through a number of different geographic institutions. Even if there are no unified boards it is likely that the various government units have some arrangement for cooperatively planning their parks. This is, indeed, the way it is done in Tucson.

As I mentioned above, there are frequently unified water and sewage facilities for quite large areas because it's cheaper that way. Mosquito abatement covers a fairly large area and you will find that there are large mosquito abatement organizations. Pollution control of all sorts frequently requires units that are larger than the individual city, but not as large as the state. In some cases units are larger than the state but not as large as the nation. There are also cases in which pollution control requires units that are larger than nations. In all of these cases some kind of agreed-upon organization is necessary.

In spite of the often unsightly appearance of the process of policy coordination, the outcome is usually quite good. Indeed, a very distinguished American political scientist, Vincent Ostrom, has devoted a large part of his life to looking at this kind of negotiation and arguing that it works well.[27]

Government pressuring government

Let us turn now to the other relations between these various government levels. First of all, they are fairly uniformly set up so that the higher levels have power over the lower levels. The second thing to be said is that the lower levels are extremely good in lobbying the higher levels to get what they want. The reason for the success of the lower level governments in dealing with the higher levels is simple and straightforward. The mayor of, say, New York City is in a very real sense speaking for the voters of New York and they vote in state elections too. He expects members of the state legislature who come from New York City to be on his side even if they happen to be political opponents of his in city politics. The governor also will need New York votes to get re-elected.[28]

[Government organizations] are seldom of such high quality that we might suspect divine intervention. On the other hand, they are also seldom seriously injurious.

This pattern persists throughout the whole of the government. The states have great influence in Washington and many of them, as well as many of the larger cities, maintain formal lobbies in Washington in addition, of course, to their representatives in the house and senate. The same is true of certain regional

---

27   His work is dispersed in many articles in many journals. I can think of no "master" article to cite, but most of his articles are worthwhile.

28   If the governor would like to become President of the United States, he will need New York City votes for that, too.

blocks in Canada, namely, the Maritimes, Quebec, Ontario, and the West.

The effect of intergovernmental pressures are most clearly seen when it comes to the shift of funds between different parts of the government. There are reasons why one would want to shift funds from one area of the country to another. In the 19th century, for example, the United States had a series of forts along the coast. These were paid for by taxes collected not only from the coastal states but from inland states, too. No one particularly objected to the arrangement for obvious reasons. The forts are mainly gone now, although it's still true that naval support facilities are all on the coast and are supported by taxes collected from the country as a whole.

Today we are more likely to talk about transfers from one part of the country to another in terms of helping the poor. The average per capita income in Mississippi is lower than that in New York. Hence one could argue that funds should be transferred from New York to Mississippi. As a matter of fact, if you look at the way the U.S. Federal Government acts, it is not obvious that this kind of transfer does in fact occur on any great scale. It is true, however, that this kind of transfer is talked about a great deal. In Canada, on the other hand, regional transfers are an important item in the federal budget and have been the cause of much strife between the "have" and the "have-not" provinces.

Even if the actual equalizing transfers are relatively small, it is clear that to some extent expenditures from the higher level organizations should not be simply divided equally among all the states. In the U.S., the Congressmen of the wealthier states, of course, disagree with this and make every effort to get it equally divided, and they're quite successful. The same phenomenon has recently been evident in Ontario, one of Canada's richest provinces, which argues that it deserves a net transfer from the rest of the country.

In general, it's obvious why local officials would prefer to have a federal government collect the taxes and then spend the money themselves. It's not obvious why the federal government officials are willing to collect taxes which will be spent by local governments. It is possible, however, that there is a sort of double counting here. Both the federal and the local official get credit for the expenditures and only the federal official is blamed for the tax. If the local officials support the federal official in return for the payment, there could be a mutual profit for political purposes.

In any event, it is clear that in recent years all over the world local governments have been able partially to transfer their tax problems to the central government. In the United States it isn't as far along as it is in, for example, England. This has been combined with considerable growth of the local government. This, in fact, probably explains it. Government expenditures that somebody else pays for are something that any official would like. The anguish officials feel when they are forced to pay the bill themselves is clearly illustrated in Canada. In Canada, the federal government shares in the cost of provincially administered education, health, and welfare. The provinces are now screaming because of a phenomenon known as federal "offloading." Having examined its finances and discovered them to be in disarray, the federal government has slowed its transfers to provincial governments. These governments had become used to the injection of federal money and were caught by surprise in the midst of ambitious social spending programs to which they expected the federal government to chip in its regular share.

Even if we temporarily put aside the problem of helping the poor, it seems likely that there will be very strong efforts to maximize central government expenditures which are beneficial to individual local governments. There is no end to the opportunities for political pressure that are generated by this kind of activity.

Conclusion

We have now finished our survey of government institutions. The reader has no doubt noticed that it's quick and, of necessity, somewhat oversimplified. Nonetheless, I think it's helpful to anyone thinking about designing a federal government to know what has been done in the past. The variety of existing governments is great. Selecting from among this large bouquet of governments is difficult. To do it, one must have some general idea of its composition.

Bibliography

Adie, Douglas K. *The Mail Monopoly: Analysing Canadian Postal Service*. Vancouver: The Fraser Institute, 1990.

Bish, Robert. "Federalism: A Market Economic Perspective," in *CATO Journal* V7, Fall 1987, pp. 377-397.

Bryan, Frank and John McClaughry. *The Vermont Papers: Recreating Democracy on a Human Scale*. Chelsea, Vermont: Chelsea Green Publishing Co., 1989, pp. 308, 100-200. A model for structuring government units into smaller units. This model, the authors feel, would represent individual interests and allocate public goods more efficiently.

Dye, Thomas R. *American Federalism: Competition Among Governments*. Lexington Books, 1990, pp. xvii, 219, 1-13. Definition of federalism, models and brief descriptions of federalism.

Hamilton, Alexander, John Jay and James Madison. *The Federalist*. Edward Mead Earl (ed.). New York: Modern Library.

Kohr, Leopold. *The Breakdown of Nations*. New York: E. P. Dutton, 1978, pp. xxi, 250 (originally published in 1957), pp. 170-187.

Chapter 7:
Some Myths about
Efficiency

This chapter is devoted to dispelling two important myths about modern government. In both cases the myths are also applied to institutions other than government: business, law, medicine, etc. But this is a book about government and we will talk mainly about their role there.

These two myths are first, that large organizations are more efficient than small ones and second, that the modern world is so complex that large organizations are necessary. The conclusions that we will draw with respect to the first are that there are some situations in which large organizations are more efficient than the small and other situations in which small organizations are more efficient than large.

With respect to the second, we will argue that large organizations have considerable difficulty in dealing with complex situations, although it must be admitted that small organizations have difficulty, too. Complex situations are just plain difficult. On the other hand, it is by no means obvious that the world faced by a citizen today is any more complex than that faced, let us say, by

Caesar Augustus when he sent the word down "that all the world should be taxed." The complexities are different but it is not obvious that they are more severe.

Contracting out

Let us begin with the size problem. In the first step, I would like to suggest that you think back over your last few airplane trips, and ask if you have looked out of the window and observed the trucks running around the field putting food aboard the aircraft. If you have, you will have noticed that a good many of them have something like Marriott or Trust Hotels Forte, or some even more obscure title, on the sides of them. Admittedly the Marriott chain is a pretty big chain, but it is nowhere near as big an enterprise as a major airline. Further, the Marriott chain is essentially a franchise operation[29] which means that they themselves are devoted to decentralization as a method of getting efficiency.

Nevertheless, generally speaking, those very large organizations, the airlines, find that it would be inefficient to provide their own food rather than contracting out for it. They could easily be larger than they are now, and would be if they could make efficiency gains from size and hence make more money than the smaller firms that provide the food in those odd looking special trucks. But in this case there are more diseconomies of scale than there are economies.

If you look over the western economic environment as a whole, you find this same mix of large companies and small companies. At any given time there is likely to be some general trend in the sense that companies are tending to integrate or they're tending to disintegrate. At the time of this writing, "downsizing" is all the rage and companies are reducing their

---

29   They own some of their hotels.

staffs, subcontracting out, etc. Leveraged buyouts almost always involve selling off part of a large company so that it is smaller. But that is just the trend now. I don't want to predict with any degree of certainty what the trend will be at the time you read this—for all I know that could be a time when they are growing.

In many ways, the most thoroughly integrated company, and the largest one that ever existed, was Ford in the early 1920s, when it was making an astonishing percentage of the world's automobiles. Ford owned his own iron mines, the ships that carried the iron ore to the River Rouge, the steel plant, etc.

General Motors, at the beginning a much smaller company, bought many of its components. They still do. To this day the frames of General Motors cars are made by an independent company. As a result of the competition between Ford and General Motors, Ford had to make drastic changes in its method of doing business. General Motors, of course, is now much bigger than Ford, but it has always had a rather decentralized pattern of control.

. . . two myths are first, that large organizations are more efficient than small ones and second, that the modern world is so complex that large organizations are necessary.

The same pattern can be perceived in government. When I was in college, I was told by many people that nations would grow larger simply because of the big fish swallowing up the little fish. My reply was to point out that in some cases the small fish were gobbling up the big fish, for example, the Austro-Hungarian or Turkish Empire. The advanced thinkers apparently thought that I was just one of these stupid people who could not understand things. Since that time the gigantic British and French empires have disintegrated and the certainly large, if not gigantic, empires of the Netherlands, Belgium and Portugal and Italy are gone. The tiny empires like those of the Danes and the Spaniards are also "one with Nineveh and Tyre."

When you look at governments in general, the same pattern exists. Napoleon said: "God is on the side of the big battalions." It is certainly true that there are pronounced economies of scale in military matters. A good big army will usually beat a good small army. Nevertheless, size is a long way from being everything. Even in war, big armies don't always win. Henry V was outrageously outnumbered at Agincourt, while Robert E. Lee won each of his victories against a numerically superior enemy. Eventually, of course, the numerical superiority of the Union armies simply became too much and Lee was beaten.[30] So I think we have to concede that size is important in military matters.[31]

Even here, however, both the United States and Switzerland have delegated a good deal of responsibility for military matters to local government agencies. Militia in the United States, and almost the entire conscript army in Switzerland, are to some extent under the control of the states (in the United States) and the cantons (in Switzerland).

If we move away from military, economies of scale in government activities become either small or vanishing. I earlier mentioned water and sewage as an area where there appear to be quite considerable economies of scale and hence fairly large organization may be necessary. "Large" in this case, however, means a sort

---

30   The replacement of the earlier generals by Grant was an important variable too.

31   Military size may involve equipment as well as manpower. The Allied forces in Desert Storm were quite heavily outnumbered by the Iraqi forces, but their great superiority in equipment more than compensated for that.

of confederation of cities, suburbs, etc. that are located right next to each other.

In economic systems in general, what we observe in all highly developed economies, and what we probably will shortly observe in those rapidly developing economies located in what used to be called "real existing socialism," is a wide diversity of size. There are some large enterprises and some small enterprises.

Further, this difference in size does not appear to be entirely a matter of economies of scale. There is one very large corporation called IRA which simply handles, on contract, a very, very large collection of different geographically separated food preparation and building maintenance operations. In this case, it does not appear that there are any true economies of scale, it's simply that there were a couple of people who were extraordinarily talented in running this kind of thing and they spread their resources over a very large number of units.

On the other hand, there are places where economies of scale are genuine. Most petroleum companies are large and petroleum refineries are, by almost necessity, large. Retail establishments are normally small. Chains are frequently, although not always, franchised. Historically, there has been a great shift from size to size in the market part of the economy.

IBM, Northern Telecom, Texas Instruments and, for that matter, Hewlett Packard are big companies, although neither Texas Instruments nor Hewlett Packard is anywhere near Northern Telecom's or IBM's size. On the other hand, very small companies are common in their particular industry, and in a way the present gigantic expansion started with small companies. The economy has been referred to as a "perpetual gale" in which companies rise and fall, increase in size and shrink, etc. But we do not see any necessary connection between large size and efficiency.

Probably the most powerful corporation that ever existed was the Honourable East India Company, and its Dutch counterpart was probably the second most powerful. Both of these, of course, were to some extent governments as well as trading companies. They are now long gone and were never noted for efficiency. What we have seen for a long time now is a mix of different sizes of companies in different parts of the economy. There are no doubt economies of scale in some places and diseconomies of scale elsewhere. Sometimes highly intelligent managers succeed in building large enterprises where there really is no economy of scale except the economy in making use of their managerial talent.

Size and monopoly

The argument from alleged economies of scale is frequently pushed by businessmen themselves and in most cases where this is so, it will usually be found they are attempting to obtain a monopoly of some sort. It is hard to get a monopoly in an open economy and even harder to maintain one unless you have government protection. Nevertheless, there seems no doubt that some mergers, with their concomitant increases in size, come not from efficiency considerations but from the hope, frequently not realized, of monopolistic gains. It's easier to get quiet agreements not to compete very hard if the number of parties in a given market is limited.

This is not to say that a market is highly cartelized or anything like it. It is simply that frequently arguments for mergers or expansions of companies which are alleged to be caused by efficiency are in fact excuses for efforts to get monopoly gains. In most cases this activity turns out to be harmless because the monopoly gain evaporates very quickly. But the language used sometimes convinces some people that economies of scale are much more prevalent than they actually are.

There is much more centralization in governments than in the economy. This is in spite of the fact that there do not seem to be any very obvious economies of scale outside of a few special areas like the military and, possibly, diplomacy.

For a long time the largest single activity of American government taken as a whole was elementary education. This was carried on entirely by a whole collection of very small school districts. It is now a local function, but local has changed its meaning and the school districts are much larger than they were. This seems to have coincided with a sharp deterioration in the amount that the students learn. It is not obvious that this centralization is the cause of the deterioration, but it is clear that the sharp trend towards more expenditures per pupil and a higher degree of centralization coincides with a trend towards the student learning less. Easton (1988) has given a good description of the same phenomenon in Canada. Most of the reformers today are trying one way or another to reduce the degree of centralization in the school system, although whether this will have a positive effect or not I do not know.

> *The economy has been referred to as a "perpetual gale" in which companies rise and fall, increase in size and shrink, etc. But we do not see any necessary connection between large size and efficiency.*

Looking at the rest of the government, there are few if any economies of scale. Road building, for example, is normally contracted out instead of being run by a central organization in the United States. Minor road maintenance is very commonly done directly by governments, but almost uniformly by local or state governments. Further, a great deal of that also is contracted out. Our major national highway system, which is very convenient, was funded by the Federal Government, but all of the roads were actually built by private contractors under control of state or, in some cases, even more local government units who received the funds from the Federal Government.

If there are few or any reasons for believing that there are economies of scale in government, it is clear that there are some economies of monopolization. Now I have to be careful here because it is not absolutely obvious that the particular kind of monopoly I am thinking of is a bad idea. The gains from monopolization in government are two. The first of these is that it may be easier to collect taxes if you deal with a larger area. That seems to me an issue which has to be thought of carefully and is not necessarily an undesirable feature of consolidation.

Government monopoly and information

The second characteristic of monopolization of government is that it prevents people from making comparisons or voting with their feet. If there are a lot of small government entities—school districts or direct city or county governments maintaining schools—then most of the citizens will have at least some basis of comparison. They have friends whose children are going to another school system's school, they read the newspapers about the budget, etc. This puts a great deal pressure on the bureaucrats running the system. Normally this pressure is in favour of efficiency.

To a large extent, the consolidation of school districts seems to have been simply an effort to deprive citizens of the possibility of making this type of comparison. Needless to say, that is not the explanation that was offered by people who are running the schools and who are the principle proponents of this kind of integration. Nevertheless, it did make their jobs easier in that they no longer have to continuously explain to irritated mothers why little Johnny is well behind his friend Freddy who happens to live across the border and is taking classes from another school district. Perhaps the most striking example in North America of the central school bureaucracy trying to eliminate comparisons is in British Columbia, where the province is on the road to eliminating grades and report cards for students between grades 1 and 10.

One peculiar characteristic of American and Canadian school systems is that in general the allocation of the student to the school is entirely geographic, with the parents being compelled to move if they want to change the school their child attends. This is bureaucratically convenient but it doesn't seem to have any other advantage.[32]

Clearly this aspect of monopolization by central control is something we should be opposed to. We need popular control of the bureaucracy. A larger bureaucracy is intrinsically harder to control. Individual members of bureaucracy are much more capable of avoiding responsibility for things that go wrong in a large area than in a small. The old-fashioned system in which there was a principal of the school who reported to a board of education which supervised perhaps two or three such schools was one in which responsibility could be easily allocated to the appropriate person. The New York School Board or the British Columbia Ministry of Education, with their thousands of bureaucrats, are at the opposite extreme.

---

32   American schools frequently send buses out to collect their students and bring them to school. It would, of course, be much more difficult if the students were not concentrated around the schools but this rule under which you must go to a school designated by the school board existed long before the bus route. Further, it is not possible today for a parent who wishes to move her child to get permission even if she provides the child's transportation. However, the system is beginning to break down.

Government monopoly, taxation and free riders

Another aspect of monopolization is the tax problem, which is much harder to analyze. It is perfectly possible to argue that a good deal of centralization of taxes is necessary to avoid people being free riders on the government. Getting various government services and not paying for them is obviously sensible. In any event, my own payments will be such a small part of the total that making them will hardly increase my services at all.

Consider two historic examples: the United States under the Articles of Confederation and Switzerland before the conquest of the country by the French Republic. In both cases there were a collection of local governments with a sort of nominal federation, but the nominal federation had no tax-raising capacity. In both cases there were serious military problems. Over many generations Switzerland had been a sort of protectorate of the King of France (their mercenaries provided one-third of his army). Under this protection the Swiss had acquired a very large amount of wealth, in particular the gigantic gold horde in Berne. The French Republic decided it wanted that wealth and invaded.

> *... monopolization by central control is something we should be opposed to. We need popular control of the bureaucracy.*

In both of these cases defense became impossible because each of individual states in the United States or cantons in Switzerland realized that its contribution to a military defense would have relatively little effect on the total success or failure of a defensive war. Each decided then to free ride on the "public good" provided by the others with the result that the military machine was very slight indeed.

These examples buttress the so-called free rider argument which is used by economists to justify government as a whole. (As a result of its historic origins, it is usually referred to as the prisoner's dilemma.) There are many functions which benefit everyone but in which the individual can free ride. It is easiest to understand governmental terms if we talk about national defense.

The point of taxation is to avoid this kind of free rider problem. We do not give individual citizens the right to choose to pay their share of the police force's expenditures. If we did, we can be fairly confident that the police force would be very much smaller than it is now.

Optimal size of the taxing authority

This problem raises the issue of what I have referred to above as monopolization. What is really wanted here is a monopoly of tax collection of appropriate size. The problem is that it is not easy to decide what is the appropriate size.

There are a number of easy cases, but in general if beneficiaries of any particular government activity are located in some geographical area, that area should be taxed to support it. Indeed, in some cases there are taxes that don't fall on a geographical area but on beneficiaries. The federal government, for example, finances some of its research on agriculture by a specific tax on a particular crop with the funds then used to provide research on that crop. That particular tax collecting machine has no very tight geographic boundaries, although of course it is not true that all crops are raised in all parts of the country.

This rule of taxing the beneficiaries is to some extent carried out in the United States. I mentioned earlier that we have a Tucson Unified School District which has its own tax procedure, water and sewage is provided by an institution that charges people who consume water or produce sewage, and you'll find a number of cases of this sort of thing.

I do not argue that this is optimally done in the United States, only that there lots of precedents. Unfortunately there is still a difficulty. It is not obvious that these jurisdictions are of appropriate size. The consolidation of school districts into the Tucson Unified School District does not seem to have been based on efficiency motives, and in fact has probably reduced efficiency. Still, this particular aspect of monopolization is clearly something which we cannot wholeheartedly oppose. We should agree that we should not be permitted to free ride on others' expenditures.

Note that as a general principle this is very hard to apply. In chapter 8 we will explain how, through something called "a general purpose representative," people can have considerable control over quite a large number of overlapping specialized jurisdictions without too much strain on their voting or information gathering capacities. For the present, however, I will leave the control problem aside and consider the use of taxes for another purpose: to transfer funds or resources of one sort or another from one group of people to another.

Most American cities are surrounded by a cluster of small government units or county areas in which significant population lives. Further, the bulk of this population's economic activities is either carried on in the city or at least is heavily influenced by the existence of the city. They do not, however, pay city taxes. They pay taxes in their own little suburb or county. This has led to a move to consolidate these areas into a large metropolitan area of government.

There are two reasons why we might want to consolidate. The first would be that these outer areas might be free riding on the city. This is usually put in terms of their getting city services while not paying the taxes for them. The degree to which they do this is not at all clear. If they have businesses in the city or if they do their shopping in the city they already pay a tax. The tax is, of course, not as high as it would be if they also lived in the city, but on the other hand they do not put as heavy burdens on the city as they would if they lived in it. In particular, schooling for their children, building and maintenance of their roads, and their police protection on the whole are all taken care of by the little suburb in which they live.[33]

People move to the suburbs because they are willing to pay for better services, particularly better education for their children. Once again, the American tax system comes in here. The wealthy family who might normally send their child to a private school will, if they do so, not be able to deduct the tuition for income tax purposes. If they move to a suburb that taxes them heavily and spends the money to provide a very good school they will be able to deduct it.

Many people are willing to make sacrifices to raise their children but are unwilling to make sacrifices to raise other people's children. They move into these specialized suburbs until their children get out of high school and then they move out.

So it is an empirical question whether such free riding is going on, and requires consolidation to eliminate it. This, in any given case, is normally a matter of detailed calculation. My own impression is that the suburb dwellers normally, in fact, pay as much or more in the way of taxes to the city as they add to their cost, but that's merely an impression. The calculations necessary to prove it one way or the other would be difficult, and have not been done.

---

33   As a matter of fact, almost without exception the little suburb provides better service than the city, a fact which has been demonstrated by a large number of graduate students working under the supervision of Elinor Ostrom. This work is summarized in the book by Bish in the bibliography of this chapter.

A further reason for wanting to consolidate, and this is a reason that is never mentioned publicly but I'm sure is very important in the minds of the bureaucracy and at least some of the voters in the central city, is a desire to transfer funds from the suburb to the city. This is a straightforward monopoly argument. It is of the same nature as the motives which may lead companies to merge in order to obtain greater revenue by raising prices.

If this is the motive, and frequently it is, there is obviously no reason why we should favour such consolidation. We may (in fact most people do) want to help the poor and certainly some suburbs are wealthier than their central city. Consolidation, which generally means that a lot of central city civil servants have higher salaries, is not an efficient way of helping the poor. A tax on all of the well-off people both in the city and in the suburbs for the purpose of making payments to the poor is the appropriate method here.[34]

It is interesting that this particular type of argument is never used with nations. I live in Tucson, which is a wealthy city within about 100 miles of the Mexican border. We in fact have a large number of illegal Mexican immigrants in the city and they, for the most part, are less wealthy than the rest of us. The really poor people around here, however, live south of that arbitrary line on a map. Those people who feel that we should help the poor by consolidating all the suburbs into a metropolitan government never suggest consolidation with Mexico to help even poorer people. If they really believe in economies of scale and/or if they really believe that consolidating wealthy and poor areas into one

---

34   Since I have written two books on income redistribution, I'd like to refer the reader to them rather than talk about the matter more here. The two books are listed in the bibliography of this chapter.

government is a way of helping the poor, they should be in favour of that.[35]

So much for the myth that large governments are always and everywhere more efficient than small ones. In this area I think we have to accept that, as in the economy, for some tasks large organizations are desirable and for others small. A mix of governments like the mix of enterprise sizes is what we should aim at.

The point of all of this is that the existence of uniform economies of scale is a myth. But I have not provided a rule as to the actual size of various government activities. The problem here is that not only do different government activities have different optimal sizes depending on local conditions, but the whole thing changes from time to time due to technology. I can only recommend that decisions of this sort be carefully calculated, taking into account externalities, and that the people calculating it avoid any mythological feelings of universal economies of scale.

Dealing with complexity: is size the answer?

Let us turn to the second issue, which is the view that the complexity of modern life requires large governments. I have never been able to get anyone to explain exactly what this means. They are apt to point out simply that there are many things in the world today that were not in the world 200 years ago. This is undeniably true but it's not obvious that this makes the life of an individual or government unit more complex. Indeed, it may make it much simpler.

---

35 There are no data on the subject, but it seems highly likely that almost the entire northern half of Mexico (rather thinly populated because it is desert) would vote overwhelmingly to join the United States if given an opportunity. A large part of the population sneaks across the border to get jobs in the United States anyway, and they make every effort to convert their illegal to legal status.

We have just finished the Iraqi War, in which the higher commanders had instantaneous contact with all of the lower units that they wished to speak to. Consider the situation of Lord St. Vincent in the admiralty in London in the summer of 1804. He knew that Napoleon had organized a large army and was waiting across the channel to invade England. He further knew that the French fleet at Brest was making very obvious signs of coming out to bring Napoleon across. He received a dispatch saying that some two weeks before (information was slow in those days) the fleet then in Toulon had given Lord Nelson the slip, gone out into the Atlantic and disappeared.

It took a couple of days for him either to get a message to, or to get a reply from the Brest fleet, and even that depended on the direction of the wind. Nelson's fleet, which was out of contact with Villeneuve's Toulon fleet, could be reached only very uncertainly because a dispatch boat sent out would first have to find it. If one of the English warships saw the French fleet, it first had the problem of escaping before it was captured, and second several weeks probably before it got to England.

There were also the Spaniards, who had a large fleet allied with France. If the French and Spanish fleets were going to unite forces they would substantially outnumber the English. Twenty years before, a combined French and Spanish fleet had driven the English navy out of the English Channel. At that time there had been no Napoleon in France so England had not suffered greatly from this, but now it would be a matter of great importance.

It is very hard to argue that Lord St. Vincent's problems were simpler and less complex than those facing General Powell during the Iraqi War. Further, compare the commander of an American aircraft carrier with the commander of a three-decker in Nelson's navy. The carrier has all sorts of complicated devices on board, but in general it is the duty of somebody else to see to it that they work. There is a division of labour here. The actual operation of a carrier is almost certainly much easier than the operation of a three-decker. The three-decker was an extremely unhandy ship which in combat was required to sail very close to the ships ahead and behind while being fired at by enemy cannon at short range. The ship itself was made of wood with no protection whatsoever from a cannon ball. Keeping the ship in line under cannon fire, which among other things damaged the rigging, was an extremely difficult task. To a considerable extent it was the direct responsibility of the captain. Once again, I don't see why the modern activity should be regarded as more complex.

But even granting that modern activity is more complex, it is not obvious that large organizations handle complex matters better than small ones do. About 10 years ago, MITI started to organize a massive organization in Japan to put the Japanese computer industry a generation ahead. They were going to leapfrog IBM, Texas Instruments, etc. Today[36] they are dismantling the project. After the expenditure of a great deal of money and coordination of all of the major Japanese computer firms, they find themselves still behind. *The Economist* felt, however, "that the money has not been entirely wasted. Corporate Japan has kept a foot in the door of 'massively parallel' processing, allowing it to look on with understanding as dozens of young American firms with novel computing inventions have scampered off through the doorway and down various passages."[37]

Probably the large computer and now, of course, the parallel processing devices, are the most complex single devices that are made today. They have not been developed by the monster

---

36   This paragraph is largely based on an article in *The London Economist*, "Science and Technology: The Generation Game," May 11, 1991, pp. 81-82.

37   *Op cit*, p. 81.

companies, the Japanese government and its computer firms acting as "corporate Japan," IBM, Texas Instruments, or Hewlett Packard. In general it is the small, independent companies that have produced these big devices. Cray is not a big company by the standards of the computer industry.

Another "cutting edge" of modern science, and an area which certainly is extraordinarily complex, is genetic technology. Once again, this is not a gigantic project but a vast collection of small organizations. Even the American government's current project to study the human DNA is largely going to be factored out to smaller enterprises. Complexity does not necessarily lead to large size.

I do not wish to argue that all complex activities should be carried on by small enterprises. The construction of a Boeing 747 is a pretty complex task and it is done by a very big enterprise. It is probably not as complex as building a Cray computer, but still it is a complex task. In one case, the development of parallel processing, artificial intelligence, and so forth, the actual operating units tend to be quite small. In another complex area they are large.

Even if one thinks the world is more complex
than it was before, it does not follow from
that that large governments are most efficient
for every single task.

The reason that Boeing is big and so many parallel processing companies are small is not really that complexity requires a large plant. Getting any kind of mass production at all with its attendant economies, for something as big as a 747, requires a large plant.

Altogether, the complexity of modern life, in my opinion, is greatly exaggerated. My great grandfather, when he decided to go from Scotland to Illinois, faced a massively more complex task than I will face next week when I go from Tucson to Genoa. In part this is because of the modern economy. I can use the division of labour and have other people perform many of the tasks. I make a telephone call, give my credit card number, and get to the airport in time to catch the plane.

But the same could be said for my great grandfather. He knew nothing about navigation, he couldn't build a ship and he certainly did not have all the necessary skills that were used in transporting him to New York where he disembarked and then on to Chicago.[38] Division of labour is very old. We have carried it to a higher level now than ever before, but that is no reason to believe that this means our lives are more complex. It seems to me that they are not only much more luxurious, they are also simpler.

Even if one thinks the world is more complex than it was before, it does not follow from that that large governments are most efficient for every single task. It does not even follow that large governments are more suitable for highly complex tasks like developing a parallel processing computer, as MITI found out.

In addition, many of the functions carried out by the national governments are not very complex. About a third of the federal budget goes to old age pensions, medical payments, and a few other social welfare activities. The are expensive, but they are certainly not complex. It's mainly just a computer mailing out checks. The actual provision of the medical services can be quite complex, but that is done by various smaller organizations, hospitals or even individual doctors. The part of the operation that is centralized is the simplest portion.

Another expensive activity of most modern governments is paying interest and refunding their debt, not a particularly complex activity. The final large scale government activity which in

---

38   He walked from there on and presumably understood that.

the United States and Canada is carried out almost exclusively by small local governments is, of course, education. Once again the complexities are handled at a local level.

With none of these activities can you argue that the central government should handle them because they are complex, although there may well be other reasons why they should be handled by the central government. If we turn to things like foreign policy and the military affairs, there are good reasons why the central government should run them. In both cases they are quite complex, but it is not complexity that leads us to resign them to the central government. In both of these cases there are very significant economies of scale although the American Department of State certainly does not succeed in taking advantage of them.

Conclusion

Once again, what we need is a mix of large and small governments with various governments being selected as suitable for various particular tasks. People who argue for large governments sometimes honestly think that they are required for efficiency, but far more commonly they think that large governments are necessary in order to make the transfer of funds from one area to another easier. This is sometimes true, but we must then inquire whether we want that transfer of funds. That query will be taken up again in chapter 8 of this book.

Bibliography

Bish, Robert L. *The Public Economy of Metropolitan Areas.* Chicago: Markham Rand McNally, 1971. A good general discussion of matters in this chapter as well as others.

Easton, Steven T. *Education in Canada.* Vancouver: The Fraser Institute, 1988. A good survey of the problems with state controlled public education in Canada.

Kohr, Leopold. *The Breakdown of Nations.* New York: E. P. Dutton, 1978 (original published in 1957), p. 250.

Krohm, Gregory C. "An Economic Analysis of Municipal Annexation Policy." Blacksburg: Virginia Polytechnic Institute, 1973. A doctoral dissertation, but worthwhile.

Tullock, Gordon. *The Politics of Bureaucracy.* Washington D.C.: Public Affairs Press, 1965, pp. 16-32, 120-220. The structure and operation of bureaucratic organizations is discussed and critiqued, followed by a theory of how to make bureaucracies work.

Tullock, Gordon. *The Economics of Redistribution.* Boston and Dordrecht: Kluwer-Nijhoff Publishing, 1983.

Tullock, Gordon. *Wealth, Poverty, and Politics.* Oxford: Basil Blackwell, 1988. Both of these books are readily readable discussions of aid to the poor and other kinds of redistribution.

Chapter 8: Intergovernmental Bargaining and Other Difficulties

THIS BOOK ARGUES THAT FEDERALISM is better than centralization. In order to make the contrast clear, we will begin with a short discussion of centralized governments. The first thing to be said about a highly centralized government is that of necessity a great many decisions must be made at a low level. The higher ranking officials have insufficient time to make all the decisions about everything. Further, they also normally lack the necessary information.

Since Hayek's "Uses of Information in Society,"[39] it has been known that information problems for large complex activities are extremely difficult. Hayek pointed out that the market to some extent deals with these problems, but we are now talking about the government, and it doesn't.

---

39 See the bibliography at the end of this chapter.

If you look at any large government agency that purports to be centralized, let us say a military organization, you will immediately notice that there are a good many cases in which there is internal friction. Such difficulties must necessarily occur. It will always be true that people want other people to do more than they are now doing, and economize on their own efforts. There are several basic ways of dealing with this. Normally, if there is some conflict between two parts of a centralized organization, the first thing attempted is to negotiate it out. This negotiation frequently involves bargaining. Bargaining is not the only type of negotiation. Polite (or impolite) persuasion sometimes works. Not infrequently the matter is left unsettled, with the two organizations going their own ways. The final resort, however, (short of violence) is to refer it to a common superior.

All centralized organizations are a set of departments, each of which does its own thing. In the old days, the Department of State was sometimes referred to as "a loose confederation of tribal chieftains." There is something of this in every organization. Thus, if we consider the relationship between New York and Pennsylvania on the one hand and the relationship between the Army and the Navy on the other, it's not all obvious that the level of integration between the Army and the Navy is greater than that between New York and Pennsylvania. In both cases, there are a great many things which are dealt with entirely internally, in both cases certain conflicts which cannot be dealt with internally are simply not dealt with, and in both cases certain matters are referred to higher authority.

A general rule for lowering conflict

In organizing a hierarchical structure the basic rule of thumb is that one should try to minimize the cases in which organizations subject to different hierarchical superiors have conflicts with each other. Since one of the major sources of conflict in any organization is the conflict between individuals and groups and their superiors, this minimization can never be organized in such a way that the conflicts are zero, but there are efforts to see to it that they are limited.

In the early part of the 20th Century most large private industrial corporations were organized on functional lines, that is, there would be a sales office, a manufacturing office, a purchasing office, etc. As a result of learning more about these things, they are now mainly organized in what are called profit centres, i.e. an organization that buys raw materials, manufactures and then sells one product or line of products and the next division performs the same services with respect to other products. Normally also, simple history—what they were doing last year—is important in these organizations. This form of organization minimizes conflicts between different parts of corporations.

The example of how private corporations deal with internal conflict may, however, be of limited relevance to governments. In general, what we would like would be a system under which local governments, at whichever level, are organized so that they can deal with all the problems which are relevant in their area. We would like to design governments so that nothing in each jurisdiction slops over into the next jurisdiction. Thus there would be no conflict and no need of higher authority to make decisions on each specific task. Obviously that is what we would like, not what we will get.

The general-purpose representative

One way to deal with the problem of overlap and conflict which seems very attractive but has not been tried is the so-called general purpose representative. I live in the outskirts of Tucson and am subject to the government of Pima County, the Tucson Unified School District, a water and sewage organization and several other specialized units. The County Board of Supervisors and the school board are elected, while the others have boards which are appointed in the way which has been discussed above. They are composed of prominent citizens, not technical experts, and the reason they are not elected is simply that that would put too much of a burden on the voter.

There is, however, a way out. The area in which I live could elect a single "general purpose representative." She would sit in the "legislature" of the county and on the board of the Tucson Unified School District. These two areas do not have the same geographic scope so people that she worked with would be somewhat different.

Today the sewer and water authority and other specialized boards are not elected. It would seem sensible to switch those over to direct popular control by having our general purpose representative sit on them.

Thus, the individual voter would have one general purpose representative to whom he could go to complain with respect to almost anything that went wrong. It would not be necessary, and in fact it would not be convenient, to have the various organizations upon which this general purpose representative sat have the same geographic area or the same membership. In most cases, of course, there would be a substantial overlap from one to the other, but it would still be true that the members of these boards would be elected by the exact area served. This seems efficient, and it would not put much strain on the voter.

The geographic makeup of different governmental units can have a bearing on how much conflict exists between them. The greatest source of friction is that many government activities will not fit exactly into any of the government areas. To pick a very big one, New York City, is of course in New York but it sort of slops over into New Jersey and Connecticut. This has led to the establishment of the Port of New York Authority which, as the title suggests, deals with the port, much of which is in New Jersey and not in New York. It is also in control of the airports in the area, and a number of bus lines.

I should emphasize here that I am not arguing that giving it this widespread authority is sensible. Indeed, I think it would be, on the whole, better if they had not combined the airports. It would be necessary to some extent to combine traffic control in order to avoid collisions but that does not require the kind of control of the ground facilities they now have. Further, I see no reason why the Port Authority should maintain bus terminals, though it is true that many buses starting in New York end up in New Jersey.

Cases like this, in which different government units enter into agreements or create special administrative units, like the Port of New York Authority, Tucson Unified Schools District, Water and Sewage Districts in many, many places, and the sometimes complicated cooperative arrangements under which small town police forces will share various functions, are all normal.

These various cooperative arrangements in general are not organized simply because of economies of scale. General Motors, after all, has more economies of scale by far than does the little area around Tucson or New York. Nevertheless, it does not have this kind of geographic interrelations. In general, governments specialize in those activities in which economies come to a large extent from having a given geographic area served by the same organization. That is, of course, the basic reason why my proposed "sociological federalism" deals only with matters which have no great geographic component like marriages, family relations, education, etc.[40]

---

40   In the United States education has become geographic by way of the school boards designating the exact physical district from which people attending a given school will come. At the time of writing, this system seems to be disintegrating. People are demanding choice for parents.

There are, of course, economies of scale in some areas. We mentioned, for example, sewage disposal, but nevertheless in the case of sewage disposal the ability to lay out a continuous set of sewers is probably at least as important as the economies of scale in the actual sewage treatment plants. This is true with respect to most other functions of government.

Although this is true, there have been and are today various cases in which the geographic area seems extremely oddly-shaped. During the period in which West Berlin was cut off from West Germany, there was a small piece of West Berlin that was cut off from the rest of West Berlin by communist territory. American officers visiting it had to use helicopters. This was, of course, a hangover from an earlier period.

If you look at maps of early Germany or Italy you'll find many cases in which the Duke of such and such held quite distinct pieces of territory which were not geographically contiguous to others. An extreme case of this, of course, was Charles V of Hapsburg, whose properties in rather small pieces were scattered all over the map of Europe. His one really large area of contiguous land was the American continents where, although both were claimed by him, actual governmental control extended only over the Caribbean area and Peru.

Normally, however, the governmental units require more or less contiguous areas for efficiency. In most cases in which there are economies of scale but contiguity is not required—the General Motors model—there is no intrinsic reason why government should not contract out. This is indeed fairly common, with the contracting normally done with another government unit. I mentioned above the Lakewood plan in which Lakewood got its police work from the sheriff's office, its tax collecting from the city of Los Angeles, etc. There has recently been a drive to substitute, to considerable extent, private companies for many of these things. At the moment there are a number of private companies in the United States that are running prisons. Further, these prisons are frequently a long, long way from wherever the prisoner was arrested and convicted.

Difficulties of cooperation

When there are no economies of contiguity the problem is relatively easy because you can contract the matter out in a competitive market. Where there are economies of contiguity—the sewage system more or less does have to be run as one unit—the problem is more difficult and it is to those problems that I would like to turn in this chapter.

Suppose that we have a situation in which there are six or seven small communities which can indeed gain by establishing a consolidated sewage plant. It its almost certain that some of them will be able to gain more than others. It's also quite likely that, let us say, one or two of them could, instead of joining this consolidated sewage plant, choose to annex themselves to another one in a neighbouring area.

Under these circumstances, bargaining as to the cost allocation of the sewage plant can be quite difficult. I would advise anyone who is attempting to arrange one of these things to try and work out some simple and apparently just rule of thumb and then stick to it. For example, the sewage plant itself can be put up by borrowed funds and it would be paid for by a flat fee on the water bill so that the more you use the more you pay. There is also the fact that occasionally city governments will attempt to use their special advantages to impose this cost on their neighbours. Los Angeles and New York are examples. The city of Los Angeles, when originally set up, had control over almost all of the water sources in its immediate vicinity. Since it's a semi-desert area, there weren't very many. In general, it insisted on only distributing water to parts of the city, so if you wanted water you had to be annexed. This led to a very great growth of the city.

Eventually the state legislature put a stop to this with the results that water can be obtained by other communities in the general vicinity of Los Angeles, and now the city itself is simply a large area in the middle of a monstrous metropolitan area with many other cities and unincorporated pieces of the county surrounding it. It was a case in which the Napoleon complex by the city government had been successfully implemented for many years but eventually they met their Waterloo.

But we're not solely facing a Napoleon complex here. It isn't quite that simple. The view that large government agencies are more efficient than small and that consolidation always leads to higher efficiency is in fact quite honestly held by a large number of misinformed people. It is of course pushed with great vigour by civil servants, who expect their areas to expand, and by people who in fact are interested in transferring money from the newly annexed area to the older area. Nevertheless, many people, including Mr. Shapiro of DuPont, honestly believe that these large conglomerations are improvements in efficiency. In Canada the public takes great pride in its provincially consolidated hospital systems. There is a very powerful belief that uniting all hospitals under one central authority, instead of under county authority or even private authority, saves Canadians the costs of what they see as "wasteful competition" in the U.S.

All we can do about this mythical view of government is simply to point out that it is mythical, and to emphasize the possibility of contracting out when there are genuine economies of scale. In practice, of course, it usually turns out that some of the things that civil servants point to as economies of scales are not such economies.

Who's giving the orders?

Let us turn to the relations between the local governments and higher level governments. These again are frequently quite acerbic, but on the whole nothing very serious in the way of damage comes out of the quarrels. I've already mentioned that the higher level government contains, built into it normally, representatives of the lower level government, in the form of members of its legislature elected from local areas. Local governments also maintain sizeable lobbies.[41]

The situation is interesting because, theoretically, the higher level organizations have complete control over the lower. In fact, the voting power is such that this control is not likely to be exercised very vigorously. If I may offer a personal preference, I would like to have this complete power to a large extent eliminated. In other words, I'd like to give the local communities the same powers with respect to the state government that the state government has with respect to the national government.[42] The central state government does in fact perform a genuine service for the lower organizations in the sense that it probably makes cooperation among them a little easier than it would be if this organization were not there. The ability to refer a dispute between two neighbouring cities to a higher authority, both of the cities having their representatives in the legislature of the higher authority, is of course quite convenient. But as I have argued so far, such centralized control, while sometimes convenient, can stifle competition between governments and reduce the choices voters have.

---

41 Once again, I'd like to point out that this is not just a problem of geographic decentralization. Government bureaus in centralized states maintain formal lobbies in the court of the emperor or in the capitol building in Washington. The only difference is that they don't admit that they are formal lobbies.

42 Once again the two additional "levels" of government that I'm in favour of, neighbourhood associations and non-geographic organizations, would also have these powers.

To repeat a theme which may be boring the reader by now, as a general rule, the central authorities would do almost anything for a local government in the way of reorganization that all of the elected representatives from that local government favour. When it comes to revenue considerations, problems are not that easy.

As a general rule every local community would like to get more out of the state government than it pays in. And they will certainly try. Further, the voters and their representatives frequently work very hard for these things.

If the representatives from Tucson ask for special privileges for Tucson, in essence the only people who have the general public interest at heart are the representatives of the other cities and unincorporated areas in Arizona.[43] Unfortunately, these representatives normally have their own axes to grind and are apt to make trades.

Conclusion

This whole chapter has been devoted to discussing the problems of negotiation among the states, cities, and I hope eventually neighbourhoods. The situation is apt to look rather messy in detail and, to repeat what I said earlier, intellectuals normally get quite upset about it. The ultimate outcome, however, is usually reasonably satisfactory. Although it is not Paretian in the sense that every bit of gain which could be squeezed out is realized, it certainly does better than a large bureaucracy would.

---

43   And of course the local congressmen in Washington do the same.

Bibliography

Dye, Thomas R. *American Federalism: Competition Among Governments*. Lexington Books, 1990, pp. xvii, 219. A good reference overall to this chapter as well as others. An introduction to the idea of competitive federalism. The historical perspective of American federalism as a protection against tyranny is challenged with the idea of rival and competing interests. Dye feels that this competition is more in the spirit of the founding father's concerns for controlling the power of government.

Hayek, Friederich A. "The Use of Information in Society." *American Economic Review*. September 1945, pp. 519-30. This pathbreaking article demonstrates the extreme difficulty of obtaining adequate information in large organizations.

Ostrom, Vincent. *The Political Theory of a Compound Republic: Designing the American Experiment*. Lincoln, Nebraska: University of Nebraska Press, 1987, pp. xxviii, 240. Relevant here as well as in earlier chapters.

Chapter 9:
Technical Problems

THIS CHAPTER IS MAINLY DEVOTED to the interrelationship between different government units which, by necessity, is an
important problem in federal states. It should be emphasized,
however, that it is also an important problem in centralized states.
It's simply that the units are different. Relations between Arizona
and New Mexico are much less unfriendly than the relationships
between the Department of State and CIA. In both cases, appeal
to higher authority, as we have discussed before, tends to put too
much of a burden of decision on higher authority and hence
problems have to be dealt with locally, for the most part, with
only occasional references to higher authority.

But this particular chapter is devoted to relations between
federalized units, and not to the relations between, shall we say,
the Tucson Park Board and the part of Tucson government that
deals with the homeless.[44]

---

44 New York has recently had some mild wars in which homeless are thrown
    out of parks by late night raids carried out by masses of policemen. Tucson
    has so far avoided this, probably because there aren't so many homeless.

The problem of course is that the activities of any given unit tend to spill over into other units, whether those units we're talking about are geographically federalized ones or geographic parts of a federalized state or, a third possibility, non-geographically federalized ones. In those American cities in which the school board is a separate elected agency with its own taxes, there are various spillovers in the behaviour of the school board and the rest of the city government even though they occupy more or less the same geographic space. It should be emphasized in the first place that, as far as I know, these spillovers, although they certainly lead on occasion to a good deal of irritation and bad temper, rarely seem to lead to anything more serious once the federal system has been adopted.

The first overlap that I'm going to deal with is frequently not considered a technical matter. It has to do with helping of the poor, the sick and the elderly. Of course in many cases the reason people are poor is that they're either sick or elderly. In practice, as I hope to demonstrate below, there is no significant problem with governmental overlap in dealing with the needs of these groups, but there is a good deal of theoretical discussion of the matter. On one occasion, Richard Musgrave, a famous public finance scholar, said in a meeting (in fact, he was addressing me) that no one had even suggested a way in which aid to older people could be decentralized. Since it had been decentralized in the United States up to the mid-1930s and still is to a considerable extent, this was quite a remarkable statement. But it does reflect the present state of the theory, if not the present state of practice.

Dividing responsibility for social aid

The problems that people worry about when it comes to proposals to divide up responsibility for the poor, the ill, and the elderly in the way that it was divided up in the United States until the

1930s fall into two categories: tax revenue and actual payments. Let us begin with the payments.

It is likely that as people are charitably inclined to different degrees in different parts of the country and also have more or less money, once again in different parts of the country, local governments will choose to provide lower relief payments in some areas than in others. If the difference were sizeable people could migrate from a low paying state to a high paying state for the purpose of living on relief.

The problem was dealt with before the 1950s by simply sending them back. When a citizen of Mississippi moved to New York and on arrival applied for relief, the relief agency would simply give him a bus ticket back to Mississippi.

Unfortunately, this scheme was abolished about 20 years ago by the Supreme Court of the United States. In a decision which I personally regard as bubble-headed, they ruled that people have a constitutional right to move from one state of the union to another even if they're planning on going on relief.[45] The obvious simple solution to this problem is simply to return to the system that was customary in the United States for so many years, and that is customary today internationally.

---

45   Incidentally, although under current American court decisions you do have a constitutional right to move from one state to another in order to improve the amount you receive on relief, you do not have a constitutional right to move from one state to the other to practice your trade as an electrician. In many states there is a state-managed cartel of electricians (and other trades) which keeps their wages above what they would be in a competitive market. The cartel is operated by making entrance difficult, and the courts have held that these rules, even if applied to somebody that moved from another state, are perfectly constitutional. This is ridiculous, but one must anticipate that any government will do a certain number of ridiculous things.

The United States will, for example, refuse admittance to the country to people who might go on relief.[46] It is not absolutely clear that they will boot them out of the country once they get in, but even that is likely. Most European countries are much more stringent about this kind of thing than the United States. Canada, on the other hand, is incredibly lax. British Columbia allows Americans who enter the country to go directly on relief if they wish. This has led to a seasonal north-south migration of welfare recipients in the Vancouver-Los Angeles corridor. Similarly, Ontario is now developing an international reputation as a province that will cater to the needs of illegal immigrants, and pay their legal fees for immigration hearings which may last up to three years.

We might digress briefly here to say that most people who feel that there should be equality in the amount that poor are aided by the state regard this as only true within national boundaries. I live within about 100 miles of the Mexican boundary and the borderline between the United States and Mexico is one of the places in the world where the change in living standard is most abrupt. The average Mexican has less than ⅕ as much as the average American.

I also live in a university community full of professional bleeding hearts. Few of them, even though deeply concerned about the various poor people in Tucson, feel that the United States should make any effort at all to provide to Mexicans the kind of living standard which they think should be provided to Americans. They are more concerned with the poor people living in Mississippi than those in Mexico even though the poor people living in Mississippi have incomes three times that of those in Mexico.

---

46   The *New York Times*, July 16, 1991, has a front page story and a picture of 163 Haitians being sent back to Haiti.

Benefits of decentralized social aid

This distinction between national and local is common. If the reader feels that poor people or old age pensioners or those who are ill should be financed in the same amount throughout the country, this more or less requires a centralized system. I would suggest that people who do feel this way, however, should think carefully about why they think it should be the same throughout the country, but not across international boundaries.

The other thing to be said here is that during the period when the system was entirely local the relief payments tended to be about the same percentage of average income in any given community as they were in any other. The difference was that some communities were wealthier than others and hence had higher average incomes and so higher relief payments. It is most likely that this would be true again. Measures like internal free trade would tend to equalize incomes, and would tend to prevent these differences from being gigantic, as in fact it did under the previous system. Further, free migration from one state to another of craftsmen like electricians would also tend to equalize incomes.

In a decision which I personally regard as bubble-headed, [the Supreme Court of the United States] ruled that people have a constitutional right to move from one state of the union to another even if they're planning on going on relief.

The second problem people have with splitting power between different levels of government is revenue: it is sometimes alleged that a state which is generous in paying for the poor will, of necessity, have somewhat higher taxes. As a result it would be in a poor competitive position with other states, so the argument goes. This would of course apply to local governments as well. (Before the 1930s, relief payments very frequently were actually a local municipal or county responsibility rather than a state responsibility in the United States.)

This argument is undoubtedly true enough, but it's also fairly trivial. The total amount spent on aid to the poor is usually a very small fraction of any government's budget. The social welfare system, social security and medical payments may seem large. But a large part of these payments go to people who are by no means poor. More than half of the money spent for old age pensions in the United States (as is discussed in somewhat more length below) goes to people who are in the upper half of the income distribution. A very tiny amount goes to people who are poor enough so that they qualify for supplementary security income. In Canada the proportion of the well-to-do picking up unemployment insurance, and social security, is even more pronounced.[47]

Portable social benefits

There is a further alleged problem with decentralizing the administration of social services which comes essentially from the work of Prince Bismarck, the inventor of the modern welfare state. Most governments today provide old age pensions, medical insurance and unemployment insurance to most of their citizens. This is usually paid for by special taxes falling on the income of the employed.[48] These payments do not necessarily go to the poor

---

47   See Isabella Horry's and Michael Walker's trenchant exposé on the perverse redistributive effects of Canada's social programs in *Fraser Forum*, March, 1993.

48   In the United States we follow Prince Bismarck by making a pretence that half is paid by the employer, but no economist has been fooled. It's only the voter whom that political genius, Prince Bismarck, succeeded in deluding.

although of course as we've said above, one of the reasons for being poor is that you are sick or old or unemployed. Many people believe that without central government control, there would be too much difference in the style of these social programs between local governments, and that as a result people would be discouraged from moving between districts.

Let us take up pensions, medical insurance, and unemployment insurance one at a time. In the first place, the old age pensions raise no particular problem if they are made what we call in the United States "portable." As a simple example, I worked for a number of years for the state of Virginia in various educational institutions. As a result, I acquired certain pension rights the cost of which was deducted from my salary at the time. When I moved to Arizona these pension rights moved with me. Indeed, I am currently collecting my pension from Virginia.

Now, I will actually at various other times in the later part of my life collect various other pension payments from other employers and the state of Arizona. The difference is simply the age at which they begin making payments. All of this is perfectly simple, is required by law with respect to private pension schemes, and could easily be dealt with in exactly the same way by local governments.

Suppose, for example, the old age pensions are taken care of by city governments. Living as I did in the early part of my life in Rockford, Illinois, I would have paid the appropriate taxes there and acquired a certain amount of pension rights. When I moved, as again I did, to Virginia these would lapse for a period of time but when I became 65 I would be able to begin collecting that amount. Private "portable pensions" were originally developed before computers were available. Now with computers the bookkeeping is ridiculously simple.

Medical insurance and unemployment insurance are, if anything, easier. In general there is no large accumulation of payments over a long period of your life and then a payment out at the end. The payments come more or less randomly in both cases. It would be unwise for any local government unit to agree simply to start unemployment insurance for anyone who moved into the community the day he moved in. But anybody who came in with a genuine job could be given standard coverage without difficulty. The one who moved in without a job would be dealt with just like somebody who wanted to go on poverty relief.

More or less the same situation exists in medical care. Today New York has a very generous medical care system and Mississippi a not very generous one. There is no reason why people can't move from one to the other, because the taxes which are collected to support them will be greater in New York than in Mississippi. These taxes largely fall on the potential beneficiary. On the other hand, someone who became seriously ill in Mississippi and immediately moved to New York in order to get better medical attention should be discouraged.

With regard to revenue for these two (and for that matter, all three of these) items there is a tendency to feel that putting taxes on the workers to pay for these benefits leads to workers being unwilling to live in the places where the benefits are high. It is thus thought competition would drive the benefits down.

The problem with this line of argument is the assumption that people really do not want these pensions, medical attention, etc. The citizens in New York choose to have a higher level of medical care than the citizens in Mississippi. This is presumably what they want, and they're not likely to move to Mississippi in order to get lower taxes if those lower taxes are combined with poorer medical attention.

Decentralization helps self-selection

We would anticipate that if different cities, states, counties, etc.[49] have different levels of provisions for unemployment and medical expenses combined with different levels of taxes, then citizens would have some tendency to sort themselves out according to their preferences in these areas. It would be rather like the present situation in the United States in which there are some small suburbs with high taxes and very good schools and others with low taxes and mediocre schools.

The fact that people can "vote with their feet" and thus sort themselves out into different areas with different collections of public goods is one of the great advantages of federalism. It would apply also for medical and unemployment insurance, providing only that you could not pay low taxes in Mississippi until you got sick and then move to New York. Voting with your feet is an advantage which the U.S. possesses in reasonable measure but which its northern neighbour has been doing its best to rid itself of. There is a great push in Canada for "uniformity" of services wherever you go. This however has not led to uniformity of taxes. The poorest provinces still pay the lowest taxes. Through a collection of taxation and revenue-sharing agreements between the provinces and the federal government, there is little room for people to sort themselves out. The end result is that the wealthy pay the most for services, even if they do not consume them.

The reason all of this can be dealt with this way is simply that in the U.S. beneficiaries of the various tax expenditures are more or less the same people as those who pay the taxes. Local government units and, for that matter national government units, have to be careful that they will not tax their citizens very heavily for

---

49 It could be even my little homeowners' association at the extreme.

something that primarily benefits their people from other cities or countries.

Technical difficulties with decentralization

The matter will be dealt with in connection with specific examples below but there can be some difficulties. My little Sunshine Ridge Mountain Homeowners' Association has rather nice recreational facilities but, of necessity, it restricts the use of them to members and guests. Local government units that provide recreational facilities well above that of their neighbours should either require a fee for the use of the services or restrict them to their own citizens.[50]

There are other more or less purely technical problems caused by the existence of cities close to each other. To take one example, the introduction of modern sewage disposal occurred at a time when most sewage engineers did not fully understand the germ theory of disease. As a consequence, it led to sharp increases in death rates from diseases downstream. The sewage was characteristically simply dumped into a natural stream which meant that, for example, the yellow fever rates went up in certain parts of the United States.

This is not a terribly easy problem to deal with. As late as the 1950s American cities had periodic overflows in which raw sewage did go into streams. This was a clear cut injury for those who lived downstream.

The cause here was the fact that the cities have two sewer systems, one of which carries off sewage and the other of which is intended simply to get rainwater out of the streets after a

---

50   A combination in which the citizens get it free and people from outside must pay a fee is also possible.

thunderstorm. For technical reasons it is cheaper if these two systems are to some extent intermixed and it wasn't until the 1950s that the interconnections were finally eliminated. Thus, sanitary engineering to some extent certainly increased total threats from some diseases. The net effect, however, was no doubt to reduce death rates.

There are sometimes several government units dealing with the same stream. For example, the Rhine or the Danube in Europe or the Colorado[51] in the United States. This kind of problem is important. It has been dealt with by lengthy negotiations among the various governments involved. In the case of the Colorado, the "treaty" among the states was then formally enacted into law by the national congress.

In general such problems are best dealt with by this kind of negotiation between government units. The Ruhrgesellschaft is a good example of a complex set of bargains among a number of government units and, for that matter, private companies within West Germany which resulted in an organization which is widely believed to be a model for other similar areas to imitate. All of the small government units that are involved with a given stream or water course[52] may prefer that the central government take control of these areas. Indeed, in such a monster watercourse as the Mississippi Basin, this may be the most efficient method.

Normally, however, detailed negotiations among the local governments are apt to produce a better result than central government. In any event, as we have emphasized again and again, it is unlikely that central government will make any serious effort to impose its will on the local governments in a democracy. The

---

51   Pollution is not the main problem with the latter. It flows through desert areas and the use of the water, which is highly valuable, is disputed among the states.

52   Sometimes subsurface water sources.

voters who elect the local governments also elect representatives in the higher level legislatures.

Air pollution raises somewhat similar problems. As a general statement of technology, the air pollution problem seems to be either quite local or very general indeed. The Los Angeles Basin is an example of a quite local and very severe air pollution problem. The possibility of global warming[53] from carbon dioxide surely cannot be dealt with locally. There don't seem to be many intermediate cases.

In the United States, in any event, a good many of the air pollution regulations have been unwisely moved up to state or national governments where they should not be. It would be even better to have the matter done on a strictly local basis, with the local politicians taking into account both the cost and the benefits of pollution reduction.

Once again, if local governments do make these arrangements, they will probably have little difficulty in getting a higher level of government to ratify them. In the United States, the environmental movement has had great difficulty in dealing with local governments, who take careful account of both the benefits and cost of pollution. In consequence they have very largely concentrated their attention on the federal government. It is hard to avoid the conclusion that the local governments do better here although if you are a fanatic green you may feel that people should be prevented from breathing because breathing produces carbon monoxide.

Both water and air pollution are clearcut cases where government action is called for and where the government action frequently requires more than one government. Whether these are nations as they are on the Rhine and Danube, states as they mainly

---

53   Personally, I think the possibility is a weak one. I could be wrong, however.

are on the Colorado, or local governments in some conurbation, it is still true that the area which must be controlled is normally not exactly coterminous with government boundaries.

Thus bargains and negotiations are necessary and they are frequently rather slow. It's not obvious that this is undesirable, because by the time the negotiation process reaches its end science will have progressed at least to some extent and it may well be that an improved solution is available. Like most intellectuals, I tend to regard local politicians as ignorant, biased, and not overly bright. I am usually deeply astonished at how well the outcomes which they generate work.

There are other technical contacts between different communities. An obvious one is road patterns, in which the roads should meet at the borders. Once again, there is rarely any great problem about this. Individuals normally want major roads near but not too near to their homes. This leads to a good deal of ill temper but normally some kind of solution is worked out. Certainly it's very rare indeed for two communities to build segments of a main road which simply stop at the border of each one because they have not been brought into contact. This is true not only with counties or states in the United States but also with nations in Europe.

Another alleged problem with decentralization has to do with the possibility of people committing crimes on one side of the border and then quickly retreating to the other. In the United States it is not a problem within the states because policemen of one part of the state have jurisdiction in others at least for arrest, but across state boundaries there were constitutional barriers.

Various informal arrangements took care of this matter for a very long period of time. One state could "extradite" criminals from another without a great deal of difficulty.[54] Today, of course,

---

54 Sometimes there was difficulty. When I was in law school I was told about a black who was accused by the state of Alabama of having committed a

we not only make use of this extradition procedure but the Federal Government also intervenes. It enacted a law making it a federal offense to cross the state line for the purpose of avoiding prosecution, and hence you violate a federal law when you do so and can be reached anywhere in the Union.

The FBI, which has been steadily growing, has put a good deal of effort into enforcing this law. Indeed it's arguable that the real function of this law is to improve the appropriations of the FBI. Internationally, there is something very similar, called Interpol, which performs much the same coordinating function. As far as I know, it works about as well as the FBI. It's about as dangerous to commit a crime in France and depart quickly for Spain as it is to commit a crime in New York and depart quickly for Pennsylvania.

Useful functions of central organizations

This suggests that central organizations from a higher level government might be convenient in these cases. It should be said that there's one other area in which it is certainly convenient. The FBI, and for that matter Interpol, maintain central information organizations which identify fingerprints, track wanted people and perform various other technical functions that would be quite expensive if performed by each and every little county.

---

crime. They attempted to extradite him from Massachusetts. The governor of Massachusetts refused to sign the papers, saying that he doubted that a black would receive a fair trial in Alabama. Shortly thereafter, Massachusetts attempted to extradite a Jew from Alabama and the governor of Alabama refused to sign the appropriate papers, saying that a Jew might not receive a fair trial in Massachusetts. The result of this was that for a considerable time if you committed a crime in either one of these states and quickly got to the other you were safe.

But to say that this would quite expensive for every county does not mean that it must necessarily be done by a centralized organization. Indeed, the FBI maintains several regional offices, rather than one for the country as a whole. Interpol also is moving in the direction of regionalization.

The potential of voluntary activities to deal with crimes or other difficulties which are too sizeable for one jurisdiction should not be ignored totally. In the United States during the riots and burnings of the 1960s, a number of local police forces made arrangements to deal cooperatively with the matter. They could concentrate forces in one city or town that seemed to be the most dangerous place. There is no reason to believe this worked less well than the highly centralized way of dealing with the same thing, which is characteristic of, say, France. On the other hand, it should be said that there is no reason to believe it worked better.

. . . governments very commonly are engaged in transferring funds from some people to others. Such transfers are hard to implement in small government units with no control over imports or exports.

In all of the above areas, it is possible to deal with the problem either by agreements among local governments or by having a higher level central government handle the problem. My own bias is towards the local government, but it should be said that is clearly at the moment more bias than anything else. If the reader prefers to have the central organization deal with these things, I can't quarrel with him terribly. He should, however, at least be consistent. If he feels that the state of California is too small a unit to deal with certain types of air pollution, he certainly should feel that Switzerland is. There is a strong tendency to think that somehow national boundaries, which are essentially arbitrary lines on the map, are part of the state of nature. In fact, they're human artifacts and don't necessarily indicate the ideal geographic structure of various government agencies.

A selection of tax systems

As a final item, I'd like to turn to the problems of having different tax systems in different areas. Traditionally in the United States local government was supported by a tax on local real estate which had the nice characteristic that since the local real estate couldn't move there was no really serious problem in one community having higher taxes than another. Each community could choose that bundle of taxes and benefits that it wished.

This was not, of course, perfect. The real estate tax was not a tax on the value of the bare land, but on the land plus the buildings. Thus a high tax might lead to people deciding that they won't put buildings in your community. To a large extent this would depend on whether the services generated by the local government were superior in heavy tax areas. Henry George's "single tax" which falls on the bare land only is theoretically better, but hard to administer.

The basic problem here, however, is not too much tax combined with too many services. It is the fact that governments very commonly are engaged in transferring funds from some people to others. Such transfers are hard to implement in small government units with no control over imports or exports. Consider a small county trying to benefit the farmers by raising the price the city dwellers pay for food. People would buy their food from outside the community.

If we consider only the aid to various special groups that were being paid off simply because they were well organized, most people would agree that competition among the states and local governments is highly desirable simply because it gets rid of such things.

There is, however, one particular area which might cause trouble: aid to the poor. It might well be that the transfer from upper income people to the poor, if it were highly generous, might lead to wealthy people moving out. As a matter of fact, it rarely is highly generous, so this is not a major problem.

A more difficult problem, however, has to do with types of taxes. Local governments should obviously be free to experiment with different taxes, and the existence of competing jurisdiction just down the street may make this very difficult. In fact, it may drive them back to real estate taxation as the only revenue source. New York City's various efforts to impose a fairly hefty income tax is an example of the problem. It has led to the migration of a good deal of business to Connecticut and New Jersey and, for that matter to Bermuda and the Cayman Islands.

In Europe, of course, the problem now that the international boundaries are being robbed of their economic significance, is in fact an international and not a local one. The Brussels organization, in its usual effort to cartelize everything it lays its hands on, is attempting to get everyone to charge the same taxes in order to avoid this kind of competition. I would regard the competition as desirable. A number of things that the governments are now doing will necessarily become impossible, and that is a step in the right direction.

Why are we centralizing?

I have been arguing quite strongly for use of local governments instead of central governments. As a matter of fact, however, in the last 30 or 40 years there has been a fairly strong tendency for the powers of local governments to migrate towards higher level governments and, in particular, for local governments to be funded by taxes collected by the higher level governments. This is as true of Canada as it is of the United States. Why is this?

The standard arguments for these movements are almost always in terms of improved efficiency. This is normally not accompanied by any positive evidence that the large governments are more efficient than small. As far as I know all the empirical studies of cases where, let's say, suburbs have been combined into cities or school districts have been combined into consolidated districts show either no change in efficiency or positive decline. From the proponents of these larger governments there is no argument except the sort of *a priori* feeling that big size is more efficient than small. They give no real evidence that efficiency would increase.

There are, however, some very strong reasons why a number of people interested in the government would want an increase in scale even granted the fact that they expected a decline in efficiency. It is normal among human beings to object to competition. Everybody wants a monopoly and doesn't want people moving to another supplier or even making remarks about how the next county over seems to be able to get its schooling done cheaper. Shifting to a larger area through consolidation or through transferring your responsibilities up does provide a certain amount of monopoly power for local government officials.

Here we must distinguish between shifting the responsibility for paying for local government activities to higher level while letting the spending go on at the local level on the one hand and actually shifting control of the whole activity upward on the other.

With respect to the first of these, the shifting of the tax responsibility upward, its advantage for local government is very obvious indeed. They are able to spend money without having to annoy their citizens by collecting it. From the standpoint of the politicians controlling the central government there is no direct advantage here, but there is also no disadvantage. They have to put up with the tedium of collecting the taxes, but the payments to the local governments appear in their political budget as expenditures. Thus they are no worse off than they would be with any other government expenditure which they must both collect and disperse.

The result is that the local politicians are made happy by this and the higher level politicians are not annoyed. Granted the fact that the central government is elected, the support of local government politicians for the members of the central legislature is always helpful and hence they are likely to regard this as a campaign advantage.

. . . in general we should aim at using the smallest government units that are feasible because, quite simply, they are more efficient and they are more under the control of the voters.

There is here another advantage which is that for various reasons taxes over large areas are somewhat less conspicuous than over small areas. This is partly because some hidden taxes can more readily be collected at the national than at the county level. More importantly, it deprives the local citizens of an easy comparison. The citizen is rather apt to notice that the next county over has a lower real estate tax or a lower sales tax. With a uniform tax collected by a higher level government, he is not provided with immediate evidence that it's possible to get by with less.

But let us consider shifting not just the revenue to the higher level but the whole functioning of some activity. I think the main motive once again is cartelist—the desire to avoid competition—but it isn't quite as simple.

Local civil servants may reasonably worry about such a change which could reduce their power, in fact might even get them fired. Local politicians will also find that their influence declines. Of course, in their case that is counterbalanced by the fact that their amount of work and responsibility also declines. This is the reason why I think that centralization tends at least to start in the form of central provision of resources for local governments rather than central government taking over an existing function.

Still, the avoidance of the possibility of comparison and other forms of competition is an obvious advantage from the stand-point of the governments involved. When local governments are pressed for financial reasons so that they have the choice between raising taxes themselves, cutting services, or succeeding in push-ing something off on the central government, they frequently choose the latter. Since the central government almost always has a motive for expansion, if one considers simply the government members themselves and not the citizenry, this is something with which they'll cooperate.

But note that I have been talking about these acts as though they benefit the government only; I've ignored the voters. To a large extent, I think this is not a bad model. The voters, when they are permitted to vote directly on these things, very commonly vote against consolidation. Normally they don't get a direct chance. In any event, the proposal for shifting the cost of the whole activity is always urged on the theory that it is efficient. If the local voter doesn't have any clear idea of efficiency and is promised tax savings, she may not object particularly strenu-ously, with the result that the activity is carried through. Indeed, local voters may be in favour of it.

Conclusion

The reader will note that I am arguing here that centralization, moving to larger government units, is to a considerable extent carried out for the benefit of the government employees and politicians and not for the benefit of the voter. I do indeed think this is true for a great many activities. There are other activities, however, which obviously require large units. To repeat, Napoleon once said "God is on the side of the big battalions" which is simply a general statement that in military matters there are very large scale economies. Centralization in that case is therefore sensible, as we have mentioned above. Air and water pollution frequently call for larger units than an individual community, although we have also pointed out that frequently this problem can be solved by local negotiations.

Nevertheless, in general we should aim at using the smallest government units that are feasible because, quite simply, they are more efficient and they are more under the control of the voters.

Bibliography

Bish, Robert L. "Improving Productivity in the Government Sector: The Role of Contracting Out" in *Responses to Economic Change*, David Laidler (ed.). Toronto: University of Toronto Press, 1986. This article would also be helpful in the last chapter but is particularly useful here. It gives a good idea of the problems and solutions and is very easy to read.

Horry, Isabella and Michael Walker. "March's solution: Effective federal spending cuts." *Fraser Forum*. Vancouver: The Fraser Institute, March, 1993.

Tullock, Gordon. *Economics of Income Redistribution*. Dordrecht: Kluwer Academic Publishers, 1983.

Tullock, Gordon *Wealth, Poverty and Politics*. Oxford: Basil Blackwell, 1987. These are books which have been cited earlier and are also of use for this chapter.

Chapter 10:
Peace and Prosperity:
How To Get Them

THE THEME OF THIS BOOK has been the desirability of decentralizing governmental functions as far as is feasible. There are
two principle arguments for it, one of which is quite simply that
the smaller units are more efficient and better able to adapt to
local conditions. The other (and frankly I regard this as more
important) is equally simple: that the individual citizens have
more control if the government is broken down into a number of
different units. Some of these units should be quite small, dealing
with problems for which they are suitable, and others quite large,
dealing with something like water pollution in the Mississippi
River Basin.

My general philosophical proposition is that government, like
any other human institution, exists to carry out the preferences of
at least somebody. It is not possible to set up a government which
does not implement somebody's preferences, although that
somebody might be Stalin. In democracy, we want the preferences of the common man to rule rather than those of a dictator

or some elite group. This book is based on the assumption that that is what we have in mind.

Governing according to the preferences of the people has two possible meanings. There is a strongly held political philosophy in Sweden which takes the view that it simply means doing what the majority wants regardless of what that is. The point of view of this book is that doing what the majority wants is frequently the rule we must follow, but we would much prefer to give each individual citizen exactly what that individual citizen wants. The basic problem that we face in government is that we can't do that except for a certain number of particular problems. Suppose then that we have some area in which individual preferences differ. That's the only kind of area we need worry about—if the individuals all prefer the same thing it will be done regardless of the form of government. Under these circumstances, the ideal thing to do is simply to give each of the individuals their own preference. It's quite possible to do this in many cases and, indeed, when we can make use of the market that's exactly what happens. Boris Yeltsin, on returning from the United States after his first visit, said it was a true worker's paradise because the average supermarket carried 30,000 different items. I don't know whether his number is exact, but it is certainly the right order of magnitude. It surely does give the individual shopper a great deal of choice.

Unfortunately, there are many subjects where the choice of one person affects others. Clothing surely not only affects other people, but probably is purchased primarily with that aim in mind. In most cases where we use the market, however, the effect on other people of individual choice is very small and we can safely ignore it. Unfortunately, there are a good many things which we can do which have significant effects on other people. The dynamiting of the Kuwait oil wells on Saddam Hussein's orders no doubt maximized his preference schedule, but its effect on other people was great and will apparently continue to be great for a number of years. Indeed it is quite possible it will have permanent worldwide affects.

What we want, then, in cases where there is a large external effect, is some kind of control under which people are compelled to follow rules that take the preferences of others into consideration as well as their own. Economists think that that is the reason that government exists.

> *In democracy, we want the preferences of the common man to rule rather than those of a dictator or some elite group.*

When we look at things which affect other people we quickly realize that the number of other people that they affect varies a great deal. Saddam Hussein's destruction of the Kuwait oil fields will have long-term effects all over the world by increasing the carbon dioxide content of the air and raising the price of petroleum. There are indeed a considerable number of other areas where local choices have world-wide effect. We attempt to deal with these by negotiations among nations, although I don't think anybody would argue that the results are perfect.

At the other extreme there are the very local kinds of externalities that I have discussed in connection with my own home in the Sunshine Mountain Ridge Homeowners' Association area. The decision as to whether we should maintain two heated swimming pools in the winter or only one affects substantially no one but members of the association.

There are many intermediate cases such as the air pollution in the Maricopa Valley or in the Fraser Valley.[55] There are a

---

55   These valleys contain the cities of Phoenix and Vancouver respectively, and because of the shape of the mountains around them, are pollution traps.

number of other areas where the external effects of people's behaviour are not of a geographic nature. Those who visit both Brooklyn and Israel will note the number of people dressed in more or less the clothing of the upper class of Poland 200 years ago. They are members of a special sect of Jews (oddly enough with its headquarters in Brooklyn, not Israel) who have very strong ideas about what other members of this little subsect should do. The rules are quite strict, but because of the nature of the Jewish religion, in which only the chosen people are required to obey these rules, they have no particular objection to, let us say, polygamy on the part of the "heretical" branch of the Mormon Church that still permits it. The rules apply only to Jews and, in particular, those in this particular sect.

In all of these cases it seems sensible to have a small government agency insofar as possible dealing only with the area where these externalities are significant. The people who live in the Sunshine Mountain Ridge Homeowners' Association bought their houses at a higher price—that is, higher than they would have paid had they been part of the ordinary city government— because they feel that the advantages of this local association are worth it. We should offer the same privilege of local self-government to other people, not only the rather well off inhabitants of the various condominium developments.

Similarly, there is no reason why the Jewish sect that I have been describing above should not be actually given some legal power over its completely voluntary membership. At the moment its members are able to exert great social pressure on deviants, but can't actually penalize them or force them to pay for the educational work of the Church by the methods that are used by other governments when a majority favours it.

One of the advantages that this system has is that although the small units are governed by majority rule for want of anything better,[56] the fact that the citizen has the additional possibility of voting with his feet is also important. With people finding it not particularly difficult to move from one government unit to another the governments are rather apt to move toward some kind of specialization. We find such things as the suburb of Los Angeles that is composed almost exclusively of warehouses or the famous New Trier school northwest of Chicago, which is maintained by a suburb with one of the highest school taxes in the world.

At the other extreme Lin Ostrom's research into police activities in small and large cities turned up two suburbs of Chicago inhabited entirely by poor blacks who undoubtedly have the most efficient police forces in the world. They didn't have much money but they had migrated out to the suburbs to avoid the crime problems of the inner city. Under the circumstance they developed superbly efficient police.

Many things can be dealt with by these methods. Tucson really doesn't have very much of an air pollution problem, but insofar as it does have one it is obvious that the Sunshine Mountain Ridge Homeowners' Association is not in a position to do very much about it. Thus a larger government is desirable for this and, indeed, for many other problems. We have mentioned at regular intervals throughout this book the problem of laying out a street pattern that it is convenient for everyone even though different people have different ideas as to how it should be designed.

These larger units do not necessarily have to be separate independent units. To some extent these problems can be dealt

---

56   Reinforced majorities or special methods of voting should always be carefully looked at in these cases. Most condominiums do require in their charter a reinforced majority for certain fundamental changes, as does the United States Constitution.

with by negotiation among the smaller units just as the pollution problems in the Rhine River are dealt with by negotiations among the nations. Most American cities are surrounded by suburbs and complicated voluntary arrangements for things like sewage disposal, schools, etc. are often found there.

Further, where you do have a complex web of different things going on, it is by no means obvious that they have to be subject to the same geographical governmental unit. I have mentioned that it is not all uncommon in the United States to have a school district with an elected board which is more or less coterminous with some regular cities. This involves, in essence, two different majority ruled organizations in the same geographic area.

Normally, when you have several government agencies in close contact there are some disagreements and negotiations among them are necessary. In general, however, things once again work best if these governments are relatively small, as small as they can be. Further, in many cases the best way of dealing with a larger problem, like sewage disposal in the Tucson area, for example, is by voluntary agreement among the various government units rather than by establishing a uniform government for the entire area. Once again, this is rather like international negotiations and like international negotiations it doesn't normally reach an ideal outcome but it does reach a satisfactory one. Indeed, as a rough rule of thumb, the outcomes are much more satisfactory when they are negotiated between local governments in the same nation simply because they don't have the strong emotional feelings that frequently corrupt international negotiations.

As the problem becomes more difficult—that is, as it is necessary to control the behaviour of more and more people in order to minimize externalities—the governmental unit necessarily grows larger. The possibility of voluntary agreement among lower level governments should always kept in mind. There are various problems which require worldwide solutions and we deal with them—not very well, but still not hopelessly badly—by international negotiations. Negotiations among governmental units within a nation raise somewhat the same problems but in general in much less severe form.

All of this is a plea for making governments as small as possible. It is also a plea for giving the common person as much control as possible over governments and making it possible for governments to be differentiated so that different people can to some extent operate under different governments, choosing which one they want by "voting with their feet."

We have talked about the problems of things like tax exporting and individual small areas attempting to develop monopoly power over their neighbours, and these do require something in the way of centralized control. Normally, however, they are minor problems and the amount of central control necessary to eliminate them is also minor. The Constitution of the United States guarantees free trade within the Union, and the enforcement of that provision has caused almost no trouble over the history of the United States. Indeed, I think most American citizens are not even aware of the fact that once in a while the federal government does take action to prevent some state or local government putting some minor restriction on that internal free trade. These things should also be minor problems for a unified Europe where the move is on towards a free internal market. The situation may be more complicated in Canada where the federal government has little effective authority over barriers to internal trade and where, consequently, these barriers exist in alarming profusion.

We want a government which is very much under the control of individuals. The smaller the government unit, the more influence any individual voter has. For every problem, therefore, we should choose the smallest feasible government. Unless we are

Swiss or Californians, we also want to economize on the amount of voting we do. Thus the number of governments we vote on must be limited, but in practice that is not a serious problem.

Experience seems to indicate that this is not only a pleasant form of government that gives people what they want insofar as possible, but is also highly efficient. Switzerland, which is the closest approximation to this that we can find in the world today, has for many generations been one of the wealthiest or possibly the wealthiest country in the world[57] despite an almost total lack of any significant natural resources and a location right in the centre of the military cockpit of Europe.

The United States, which is second only to Switzerland in its movement towards the type of government that I have described in this book, is once again either the wealthiest or second wealthiest country in the world. Further, in the case of the United States the movement towards more and more central control which has existed for the last 40 years has been accompanied by a gradual reduction in the United States' economic lead.

Further, if we look at the other really prosperous countries in the world—Canada, Australia, Germany, Japan, Sweden, Norway—we find that they either put much of their government in local units, or are very small.[58] The highly prosperous Scandinavian or low countries are so small that the individual nation is, roughly speaking, equivalent to an American state. Indeed, I would say that California is much too large to be an efficient government unit.

---

57   Their statistics are collected with the apparent desire to conceal their wealth.

58   We forced federalism on Japan after the war. Germany simply returned to its post 1870 federal traditions.

A government, then, that on the whole is under popular control and that is internally efficient can lead to very general prosperity.

The point of this book is that we can get peace and prosperity through a federalized constitution. I argue for it on grounds of efficiency, on the grounds of making popular control effective, on the grounds that it permits people to some extent to choose their own government on an individual basis, and last but not least, that it seems to work well enough so that it promotes domestic prosperity as well as peace. It is not a perfect system, of course. It will make mistakes, misjudgments, and sometimes it just plainly works badly. It's not that it's perfect, but that it is better than the alternatives.